August 29, 2011

I have known Linda Nigma for over one year now as one of her physicians.

She is an inspirational patient who made a life changing decision a few years ago. With pinpoint focus and determination she made drastic changes to her own life. At the time of this decision she was an extremely sick patient with renal failure. I venture to guess, very few would have thought that she would ever reach the point she is at today. No transplant program in the country would have thought that she would ever be well enough to receive a kidney transplant. However, despite huge obstacles, after several years of hard work and persistence, she successfully underwent a kidney transplant. The dedication that got her to where she is today is truly remarkable; however, what may be most remarkable is the positive attitude that she expresses to all those around her.

Others will be Inspired by her story. Others will learn by her example.

Marc L Melcher, MD, PHD
Assistant Professor of Surgery
Stanford University School of Medicine
Transplant Surgery

Real and Authentic Storytelling:
I know the author's family and was aware of her health condition, but reading her story was very eye opening. She is very honest about just what her fight to regain health was like. I learned a lot of details about her struggle that I was unaware of. Her story inspires me to put every effort into being the healthiest that I can be. The inspiration was much needed because I deal with a chronic pain condition every day. At times it is difficult to find the motivation in myself to continue, but then I can think of Linda and all that she has accomplished. Her goal in writing this book was to help just one person with their fight to live. I believe she has done more than help just one person.

—Ladybug

Best non-fiction book I have read 2012
I decided to wait for this book for kindle and when the announcement came out of the release. I bought it that morning. However, I wasn't able to read it until the evening and then 24hrs later after sleep, eating and work the book was done and I was inspired to change my life. The author captures you in the first few pages and the story is so moving it brought me to tears on more than one occasion. I found myself cheering the author through it all and not giving too much away. The message in the end was to be positive, chase after your dreams and believe in yourself. I have since bought the book again for my mother on Kindle.

—Roxanne W

A Fight To Live - My Amazing Journey is an Inspiring and Amazing True Story of overcoming!
My Amazing Journey is about overcoming obstacles with a positive attitude. Linda teaches us all how we need to be a self advocate when it comes to our medical treatment.

This book is a declaration and testimony about the author's life from January 2007 through October 2011 where she went from being morbidly obese, diagnosed with kidney failure and told by doctors she was going to die. A Fight To Live - My Amazing Journey details how she endured three and a half years of dialysis; lost 220 pounds and had a successful kidney transplant. A Fight To Live - My Amazing Journey is her confirmation and demonstration that a will to not give up and a positive attitude can have amazing results.

Linda confirms that she wrote A Fight To Live - My Amazing Journey to show people that you need to be your own advocate when it comes to your life. She went from a patient being told by doctors that she did not have a long life expectancy and she would die; to doing everything she could to prove the doctors wrong. My Amazing Journey shows when hardships get in the way of your life, you have a choice to confront them. A Fight To Live - My Amazing Journey also talks about giving back when amazing things happen for you. A MUST read! A Fight To Live - My Amazing Journey is an inspirational story, and as the author says, "If this book can help just one person then I have accomplished what I set out to do by writing this book." A highly intimate and brave story for everyone!

—J Weaver

A FIGHT TO LIVE

MY AMAZING JOURNEY

LINDA NIGMA

EDITORS
Susan Cox
Dianne Liebert
Patricia Perez
MaryAnn Peters

Copyright © 2022 Linda Nigma.

All rights reserved. No part of this book may be reproduced, stored, or transmitted by any means—whether auditory, graphic, mechanical, or electronic—without written permission of both publisher and author, except in the case of brief excerpts used in critical articles and reviews. Unauthorized reproduction of any part of this work is illegal and is punishable by law.

ISBN: 979-8-88640-496-8 (sc)
ISBN: 979-8-88640-497-5 (hc)
ISBN: 979-8-88640-498-2 (e)

Because of the dynamic nature of the Internet, any web addresses or links contained in this book may have changed since publication and may no longer be valid. The views expressed in this work are solely those of the author and do not necessarily reflect the views of the publisher, and the publisher hereby disclaims any responsibility for them.

One Galleria Blvd., Suite 1900, Metairie, LA 70001
1-888-421-2397

DEDICATIONS

Tim Nigma:
You took your wedding vow in sickness to a whole new level. I never would have made it without you. Thank you my Saint Tim!

Gail Bridges-Rea:
I could never thank you enough for your generosity and for giving me a second chance at a healthy life.

Joe Perelli:
Thank you for taking the time to perform the magic of teaching me to swim and helping me to reach my ultimate goal of a kidney transplant.

Dr. Marc Melcher, MD, PHD:
Thank you for being there for me both pre and post-transplant. For performing a kidney transplant that I believe in my heart no other transplant surgeon would have ever done. You are the best!

ACKNOWLEDGMENTS

Joy Allen, My family and friends for their care and compassion.

Sondra Sherwood for suggesting the title of this book. Doctors and the staff at Sunrise Hospital in Las Vegas, NV.

Kidney Transplant team at Stanford Hospital and Clinics Dr. James Lau, MD, FACS.

A Tracery of Linda

How do we trace a life on its journey toward the One?
We trace it through the obstacles that have been overcome
We trace it with the mark of love left on the lives it's touched
That tracery unfolds a heart with wings soaring toward the sun

From birth to death to life – she awakened through her pain
Reaching out with wisdom so duly earned and gained
She stood when told to lie and walked when told to sit
When death became the sentence, she surprised us all again

And now she shares her story to teach us – so can we
Become the warriors for ourselves and set our spirits free
We need to ask we need to pray we need to speak our minds
Dear Linda shows what courage is on her amazing spree

Enter gently on this journey from Sunset to Sunrise
Be prepared to see the truth that very often hides
Take a breath and welcome in the privilege of these words
As Linda shares her story and so skillfully she guides

The Beginning

Laura E Piepergerdes

CHAPTER 1

January 2007

I was trying to find out what was wrong with me for over six months. I continued gaining weight although I barely ate. My breathing was getting worse; it was getting more and more difficult to move.

My Primary Care Physician (PCP) said most of my problems stemmed from being morbidly obese and asthmatic. I also had controlled diabetes and controlled high blood pressure. For me the biggest concern was my breathing. Just to walk down the hall was exhausting.

I worked for a company as a Quality Assurance Analyst which allowed me to work at home three days a week. I went into our San Francisco office the other two days.

I would drive to the office and park next to our building, walk the half block to the doors and go to my desk on the 5th floor. By the time I arrived at my desk, it would take about 10 minutes to get my breathing settled down. Walking to the bathroom was a challenge.

Although I never called in sick, my management team realized that coming in to the office two days a week was very difficult for me and made the decision that I could work from home every day. If they needed to meet with me, we could do that in our district office in Vallejo; which made things much easier for me, because it was only 15 minutes from my home.

It seemed like I was at the doctor's office two or three times a week. It was a good thing he worked a couple of evenings a week and was less than a mile from my home. I had the same doctor for over 20 years and he could not come up with a diagnosis other than the above mentioned.

The first seven months of 2007 were challenging.

It started out with me falling down the stairs at the movies. I should say I actually rolled down the stairs at the movies. My husband, Tim and I had gone to the theater. When the movie ended I got out of my chair and misjudged the stairs and the rolling began. It was embarrassing. I didn't have the strength to pick myself up and did not want anyone to help me because I did not want anyone hurting themselves trying to assist me. I would not even let Tim help me. I rested for a while and finally got enough strength to crawl over to the seats and after resting a few more minutes I was able to get myself up. My body was banged up and bruised but not any more than my pride.

It was then I decided I had to do something drastic about my weight. No matter what I did or how hard I tried, the weight just kept going up. I made the decision to have the gastric bypass surgery. I was 5'3' tall and weighed 375 pounds.

Once I received the referral from my PCP for the surgery, it took about a month and a half before the insurance company approved the procedure. However, the only doctor the insurance company would approve was more than 50 miles away from my home.

The bariatric doctor said she wished there was something she could do for me, but until I was able to get my breathing under control there wasn't anything she could do. Not to say my breathing was bad, but you could hear me struggle with it from across a room.

The pulmonary doctor she wanted me to see was Dr. Lee, a specialist in her area; she felt if anyone could help me he could. My insurance would not cover my seeing him, but rather they sent me to a specialist that was in the same office as my PCP. The pulmonary doctor gave me 10 minutes not 11 but 10. There was never any time to ask questions. His whole way of managing his practice was he was always on time. Although I appreciated that, he was no help to me. If anything he made matters worse. My blood pressure was now out of control so he changed medications. His answer to my breathing problem was to increase the prednisone to higher numbers, then gradually bring the dosage down. The only problem with that was it shot my blood sugar levels up to over 300, 80 to 110 are considered normal. I was told not to worry, as the prednisone came down so would the blood sugar. That it did. By the way, my breathing never improved. I stopped seeing this specialist and I guess I should have stopped seeing my PCP as well. However, like a lot of people I believed that doctors knew everything.

My visits to my PCP went on and on and my health kept deteriorating. I was so frustrated by it all that it brought me to tears. I kept asking him if there was anything he could do for me. He had no answers.

I kept going on with my life, not missing work and not refusing invitations from friends no matter how I felt.

We were at breakfast one morning when our friends Dave and Dar Fray came in into the restaurant. We asked them to join us. Dar said to me at a later date, that I had looked so bad that when she went home she just cried, she thought I was going to die.

In May, 2007, Tim and I were coming home from visiting his Dad, when I noticed that the tops of my socks were wet. This was strange because I had not been anywhere near water. Then I noticed that fluid was seeping out of my legs.

We made an appointment with my PCP the next day and his answer was to take me off of a couple of medications (I was on about 15 different ones at that time) that could cause water retention. Then he said we needed to wrap my legs in gauze and ace bandages. I walked like a mummy. Tim had to wrap my legs every morning. We would go back and forth to the doctor but there were no changes. I thought I was going to die.

My friend, Sandi Rodgers is a massage therapist and she would come over to my home to massage my legs and feet to get some of the fluid moving out of my system. I had so much fluid in my feet that I could not fit into Tim's size 11 shoes.

I remember thinking that if I could only make it until my birthday then I was going to be okay. My only sibling, my brother Jim had died at the age of 53 less than two weeks before his 54th birthday. I would be 54 on May 21st.

My husband and I have the same birthday. My sister-in-law Joy wanted to have a birthday dinner for us. She would do the cooking and everyone in the family could come over to our home, which they did. My niece Seana and her husband Larry, my niece Deanna and her husband Stuart, my nephew Danny and his then girlfriend and now wife, Lynna, my Mom and Joy, were all in attendance.

What I did not know until later was that Joy had told the family (excluding my Mom) that they had better show up as this might be my last birthday. I had a lot of the symptoms that my brother had prior to his passing.

As life would have it, my Mom was the one who passed away, just four days later. Her death came as a surprise. The sad thing is even though we were at the hospital we never given the opportunity to see her before she died.

In May Tim's company officially closed and he lost his job and the health insurance that went along with it. This turned out to be a blessing in disguise, because I was able to pick up insurance through my company beginning in June. I chose an EPO. With this coverage I could see any doctor. I called and made an appointment with Dr. Lee, his first available appointment was in the first week in July.

When I went to see Dr. Lee the first thing he said to me was that I needed to have labs done and also a urinalysis. He made an appointment for the following week and asked that I bring a copy of the tests they had done for my "asthma".

I did as Dr. Lee asked and returned the next week. He first looked at the tests I brought him and said "I cannot believe this is all they have." I was told they had given me everything. He was not happy! He said he was going to have me do some extensive testing.

Dr. Lee then reviewed the lab work and had a concerned look on his face. He told me he did not like the looks of my kidney tests, and wanted to repeat this test the following week. I told him I would be out of town and could have the test done the next Friday when we returned and see him the Monday after that. He agreed but told me not to overdo things. This was the first time I had ever heard anything of concern over my kidney function. He gave me the slips for the lab work and to have the tests done for my breathing.

I never saw this doctor again.

On Sunday, July 15th, as we were getting ready to leave for Las Vegas for business I was thinking that maybe I shouldn't go. However, I knew that I had to train my new work partner, Debbie. Tim was looking forward to going and Danny was going to be there for a teacher's conference and we were going to meet up with him. So I decided to go.

I had rented a scooter from Harrah's so that it would be easier for me to get around the hotel and casino. That afternoon Danny came over from his hotel and we went out dinner at Harrah's buffet. I could not eat, everything tasted bad to me.

The next morning Tim took me over to Debbie's house so we could to work at her home office. Her bathroom was about 20 steps away from where her office was. On the way to the bathroom I had a very bad coughing attack and could not catch my breath. I sat down in the bathroom for about ten minutes. When I came back to her office I had another one and couldn't stop coughing. She asked me if I wanted her to take me to the hospital, I told her no it was just my "asthma".

Debbie fixed a very nice lunch for us but again I could not eat it. Even her food did not taste good.

We went back and worked in her office for a couple more hours and decided to make it a short day because I was not feeling good. I called Tim and told him to give me another hour as I had to finish the report on the Lake Tahoe fires before I could leave.

Tim picked me up and we went back to the hotel, but I did not want to go back to the room. I had my scooter and I wanted to play some on the machines. We played for a couple of hours and Danny came back to have dinner with us. We went to the café this time and I could not even eat the fruit salad I ordered.

During dinner Danny kept saying he did not like the way I looked. I told him not to worry; it was just my "asthma".

Tim said he wanted to play a little longer downstairs, that he would take me to the room then come back down. I told him I did not want to go to the room, I had my scooter and I would be just fine. The truth was I did not want to be left alone.

We went upstairs around 11:00 PM and went to bed. I was very restless. I would lie down and then sit back up. Back and forth I went. I got up once and went to the bathroom. I had another coughing attack in the bathroom. After a few minutes I got up and slowly returned to the bed. I sat on the side of the bed hoping morning would come soon.

I checked my blood sugar and it was higher than normal so I took my medication a little early. I checked it again a little later and it had gone up again, even after taking my medication. I knew I was in trouble. I did not want to wake Tim so I just sat there.

After a short time, Tim must have sensed something because he woke up and asked me if I was okay. I told him no. He asked what was wrong. I told him we needed to go to the hospital. He said "let me take a shower and I will go get the car and then we can go." I told him "You don't understand, I need to go to the hospital and I need to go now and by ambulance." He asked me if I was ready to hear what they had to say.

I said, "Yes, I can't live like this anymore."

CHAPTER 2

Tim called the front desk and said that I had a medical emergency. Within minutes, Harrah's medical staff was at our room. The attendants gave me oxygen and checked my vitals which included checking my blood sugar levels. They asked me if I wanted them to call for an ambulance and I told them yes. They made the call.

While waiting for the ambulance to arrive they sprayed my mouth with nitro, they thought I might be having a heart attack. During that short period of time a person from Harrah's security and the manager on duty at that time came to the room to make sure everything was going okay.

When the paramedics arrived they again took my vitals and gave me more nitro. They helped me get on the gurney and away we went.

Being wheeled through the casino was quite an experience in itself. All of the bright lights, the sounds of the machines and the people staring as I went by. I could see the curiosity on their faces. The paramedic kept reassuring me that they were going to take good care of me.

When we got to the ambulance, I heard the driver ask the paramedic which hospital he wanted them to take me to since there were several hospitals in Las Vegas. The paramedic replied "There is only one for her and that is Sunrise." As it turned out this was considered the best hospital in Las Vegas.

All I remember from the ride was that I kept getting sprayed with nitro. I do not remember arriving at the hospital, only waking up in a small room within emergency. Tim and Danny were both sitting there. They both looked concerned and more so, scared.

The nurse had just begun to put an IV in my left hand and told me they were going to insert a catheter in my bladder to start removing the excess water. They took blood from me to run a complete panel of tests.

At the time I was admitted to the hospital I was on about 13 different medications. The admitting doctor, Bashir Rashid, examined me and took away all of my medication and started me on medication they thought I needed at the time. He also ordered lab work and X-rays, and said he would be back after the test results were in.

For the rest of the day, lab technicians and nurses came in and out of the room. In the late afternoon Dr. Rashid came back in and said they were admitting me. Their initial diagnosis was:

- Congestive Heart Failure
- Kidney Failure
- High Blood Pressure
- Diabetes
- Morbid Obesity

Dr. Rashid told the nurse to arrange for me to be sent to the floor. This meant a regular hospital room. I overheard one nurse talking to the other and she said "I cannot believe he is sending her to the floor." I did not think anything about it again believing the doctor must know what he was doing.

A couple of hours later, they had a room for me. I told Tim and Danny to go ahead and leave and to get something to eat. They did not need to come back because all I was going to do was sleep and they had been there all day. Once I was settled in my room they left.

My friend Debbie came by for a short visit and brought by some magazines. When she left, I fell asleep. The nurses came in checked my vitals and the lab technicians came to draw blood. Other than those interruptions, I slept.

Around 3:00 AM, Dr. Rashid came and in and woke me up. He said he was having me moved to the Critical Care Unit. I asked why, and he said because he did not like the way my lab work came back. He indicated he thought I might be having a heart attack. The transporters came and took me downstairs to the CCU.

When I arrived, a nurse introduced herself and said she would be my private nurse for the rest of her shift and then a different private nurse would come in. I noticed the bed they had me in was an extra-large bed. The nurse told me that someone would be in to adjust the bed, it was a brand new one that had just come in and not everyone knew how to adjust it. Minutes later a young man came in and adjusted it so that I would be more comfortable.

I called Tim and told him what had happened and let him know that there was a sign in the room that said no visitors during the shift change and not to come until 8:00 AM.

Tim came in around 8:00AM and Danny a little later. My sister-in-law, Joy, called and said she was coming, Tim told her there was no need because there was nothing she could do. She said she was coming any way. She arrived in the morning and Deanna and Stuart arrived that night.

It was a day of visits by specialists. The cardiologist ordered tests and X-rays. The nephrologist (kidney specialist) asked if there had been any tests on my kidneys that showed what my kidney function numbers were. I gave him Dr. Lee's name and he was able to get the information he needed. We were not given any definite diagnosis until the next day.

When the kidney doctor came in he said my kidney function was very low and he was going to start me on dialysis. They would need to insert a catheter into my chest and I would have my first treatment later that day.

Everyone was in the room, Tim, Danny, Joy, Deanna and Stuart when Tim asked the doctor what the prognosis was. He said "She does not have a long life expectancy, she is going to have stroke after stroke after stroke and then she is going to die." I remember thinking NO I AM NOT! Someone has finally figured out what was wrong with me. The rest is just the healing process. Of course everyone else was upset.

The nurse came in and said that I had some visitors, however I could only see them one at a time and everyone else had to leave. Tim told me later he asked the doctor in front of me so it would make me more determined to fight and not give up. I told him giving up was never an option that came to my mind. Again I was thrilled that someone had figured out the problem, now we could move forward. Joy, on the other hand, was very upset with Tim for doing that.

Before my visitors came in, Tim told them what the doctor had said. All of the visitors were from the company I worked for. First Johnae (my former manager) came in. She looked at me sadly and I told her not to worry that I was going to beat this. She said to me, "I have no doubt." She offered that Tim could stay in her guest house if he would like. Next was Joey (my first manager and my good buddy). Recently he told me, when he saw me in the hospital room he thought he was going to lose his buddy. He was followed by my friend Mike and finally by Jim (the Regional Director).

Jim told Debbie to take Tim to Hertz and upgrade the car we had rented to a Lincoln Town car so that he could take me home in it when the time came. What a blessing that turned out to be. It was so nice to see everyone. Much later I realized they must have thought I was going to die because they normally do not let anyone in but family when someone is in the CCU. I found out recently that word had spread throughout the company that it did not look like I was going to recover. My, friend, Theresa Young, told me her boss, Cal, pulled her off the floor to tell her I was in the hospital and I probably was not going to make it. She told me the news had torn her up.

Later that day they took me to the operating room to insert the catheter in my chest. They decided it would be better to just take me down in my hospital bed. It was rather funny because the bed was so big it hardly fit in the elevator. The procedure was quick and before I knew it I was back in my room. Dialysis was set up for later in the afternoon.

The cardiologist came in right after I came back and said that my heart was fine and he would be releasing me from his care. This was great news because the combination of heart and kidney problems can be deadly. When my brother was diagnosed with that combination, I went to the internet and at that time it said "certain death".

They made the decision that my dialysis treatments would be in my room. When the technician came in, I told him I had no idea what to expect during dialysis. He said that for the next three hours my blood would be circulated in and out of my body as the machine filtered and cleaned my blood and it would start to remove excess fluid from my body. He told me the machine would act as my kidney. He said that it may feel weird and that I was probably going to be very tired when the treatment was over. I have always been grateful because of his explanations; I was never scared to have my treatments.

I remained in CCU for a total of six days. The dialysis treatments continued every other day.

The day came when they moved me back to the floor. This was the only time things got a little scary for me because I would no longer have my own nurse; I would have to share one. As it turned out the care was just as good on the floor. I was put in a small but private room.

The only problem was I could not eat much of anything. Nothing the hospital had to offer worked. Tim would go by Denny's, of all places, to get me a scrambled egg and an English muffin. I would eat a quarter of the muffin and a few bites of the egg and I was done. He would go out and find some of my favorites and I still could not eat.

Several of my friends from work were in Las Vegas for a Leadership Conference and came by to visit me in the hospital.

The dialysis treatments continued and there were no problems until the one night when my blood pressure dropped suddenly. The head nurse, Randy, came running in and they adjusted my bed and had my head so low that my feet seemed to be straight up in the air. I had to remain like that for 25 minutes until my blood pressure returned to normal. This is a problem that would haunt me throughout my days on dialysis.

Other than feeling weak, my spirits were high. The physical therapist had not been to see me since I was in CCU. I asked Dr. Rachid when those treatments would start again; he said he was not aware they had stopped. A physical therapist came by to see me that afternoon. I needed to get out of bed and start walking; I did not want to depend on a wheel chair to get me around.

The walking started out slowly, taking a few steps with a walker and going back to bed. Eventually I was able to take a few steps on my own; it was then that I felt more comfortable.

After nine days in the hospital, the kidney doctor came in and said I could go home the next day as long as I had a nephrologist and a dialysis center all set up to go to.

Later that afternoon, the lab technician came in and said she had to do a blood culture because my white blood count was up and the results would not be back for three days. This upset me; now there was another problem and it was going to delay my going home. The infectious disease specialist came in and said she thought they had taken too much fluid from my body, and that was what was causing the problem. She said she would be back to see me when the results were in. It turned out her diagnosis was correct. I was going to be able to leave that day. It was Friday.

In the meantime, Joy was working on getting everything set back at home. She worked with the insurance company and they said they had no dialysis centers within their network. She called my niece Seana who was the only one at home, and she was able to get the name of a dialysis center. Joy called the dialysis center and spoke with the social worker and was able to get the name of Dr. Leena Rae. Joy was finally able to get an appointment with her the following Monday. I had to see her first before I could have a treatment. She said I had to have dialysis on that Saturday. That meant another day in the hospital.

On Friday the kidney doctor came in and said that as long as I continued to lose weight I was going to be fine. He said that was key and to be sure and follow the dialysis requirements. He wished me well and I thanked him for his care.

On Saturday the dialysis technician came to my room at 7:00 AM, gave me my treatment and I was ready to go home. "Not so fast" the nurse said I needed to stay another two hours to make sure I was okay to travel. Finally at noon I was released.

The care I received at Sunset Hospital was great. They knew what to do. They literally saved my life. Dr. Rachid remained my primary doctor throughout my stay. He was wonderful. He sent me home with about half the amount of medication I had been on. One in particular stood out "prednisone". I had been taking this medication off and on for over five years for "asthma". As it turned out, *I never did have asthma.*

Part of the instructions on my release was to make an appointment with my primary doctor when I got home.

Tim brought the car around to the front exit; I was wheeled down by a transporter and got into the front seat and Joy in back. We had decided not to fly because I was too weak to sit around the airport for a couple of hours waiting for the plane to leave.

We had only driven a few miles when I told Tim I needed to lay down in the back seat, riding in the front was too hard on my back. He pulled over and Joy and I traded places.

The ride home was long but uneventful. Tim thought I should have something to eat so we stopped at Harris Ranch. I told him I would wait in the car and for him to eat something and just bring me back some soup. Joy said she would stay with me. He brought us back soup, it was good but after a few bites I was through. He was upset, because I would not eat, this was not the first time nor would it be the last.

When we got home Seana brought the wheel chair out to the car, I told her that I would rather walk to the house.

Seana had taken care of my two Japanese Chin dogs, JuJu and Kasie. I do not think she ever realized just how much stress that took off of me knowing they were being taken good care of. It was great to be home.

Now let the real healing begin

CHAPTER 3

When I came home from the hospital I was very weak. I needed help just to get out of my chair. I forced myself not to use the walker the hospital had provided. I wanted to get stronger and this was my first step toward recovery. I would walk around the house taking a few steps at a time. I would need to rest often.

Due to having the catheter in my chest, I was unable to take a shower. Tim would give me sponge baths and wash my hair in the sink. I was too weak to be able to do this on my own.

On Monday I had my first appointment with Dr. Rae, my kidney doctor. We had the wheel chair in the back of the car in case I needed it; which I did. The distance from the car to the doctor's office was too far for me to walk.

The doctor's assistant showed us to the room where I would meet Dr. Rae. When the doctor came in I was sitting in the wheel chair and had my head on the examining table. I was so weak. The first thing she asked me was if I would like some juice, I smiled and said, "Yes please."

After examining me she indicated that I would start dialysis the next morning from 6:00 AM until 9:00 AM. She said she would come by to see me once a month and I would see her nurse practioner, Theresa, once a month. She said not to worry; the center would notify her office if I was having any problems. She stressed the importance of following the special diet for dialysis patients and to make sure I did not take in too much fluid. Dr. Rae wished me well and we were on our way.

The next morning we got up early so Tim could give me a bath and help me get ready for my first day at the dialysis center. We got there early. I was told that I was to weigh in before each treatment started and then again before I left. This was how they determined how much fluid to remove from me during my treatment. In addition to cleaning my blood, the machine also removes the excess fluid. Once I was settled in, Tim left and said he would be back before 9:00 AM.

I was put in an area where I was by myself. I was given a duffle bag that had a pillow, a blanket and a headset so I could listen to the television and not disturb anyone. Each patient had a recliner with a television attached.

I met with the technician; she was also a LVN so she could attach the tubes to the catheter (only the nurse or a LVN could touch the catheter). My first day at the center had begun. My blood pressure was taken every twenty minutes to make sure it did not go too low.

I spent most of the morning just looking around and taking everything in. I noticed how bright the lights were. Some people were sleeping, some reading and others watching television. Most patients had brought food with them; they were having their breakfast during their treatment. Eating was still a problem for me at this time.

There were 24 chairs and most of them had patients in them. I had not realized there were so many people on dialysis. This center had three shifts a day. There are others that had four. One group came on Monday, Wednesday and Friday and my group was on Tuesday, Thursday and Saturday. This was only one of several dialysis centers in the area.

During my treatment, I met with the dietician that was on staff. She reminded me of all the dietary restrictions that went along with being on dialysis.

Here are a few examples:

- Eat a lot of protein
- Keep milk products to a bare minimum
- Potatoes were allowed as long as they were leached (cut up in thin slices and soaked in water for a minimum of four hours).
- No oranges but tangerines were allowed
- No nectarines but peaches were allowed
- Most important very little fluid intake

Twice a month lab work was done; phosphorus, calcium, potassium and protein were studied. It was very important to me that my numbers be within the safe zone. If my phosphorus and calcium numbers were too high my blood could crystalize. If my potassium was too high it would make my legs very weak. My lab results were always good with one exception; my protein was never high enough. I had this problem the entire time I was on dialysis.

When my first day of dialysis was complete, Tim helped me to the car and we were on our way home. I remember feeling exhausted.

On my next dialysis day they moved me to a new chair where I met Aileen Allen. She sat in the chair next to me. Her husband Chuck stayed next to her during her entire treatment. They took me under their wing. It made the time go by faster. Dialysis can be a very long three hours.

In talking with Aileen I found out that she came in four days a week for two and a half hours. She told me there was one patient there that came in four days a week for five hours. It all depended on what your body required. I was feeling fortunate with the time I needed to come in.

Following the instructions I was given upon being discharged from the hospital, I called and made the appointment to see my PCP.

I arrived at the appointment with one mission in mind, to find out how I could have kidney failure and my doctor not know. In the middle of his examination I asked him that exact question. His response was that he did not know why he had been unable to diagnose the problem. If he could not determine that I had this disease then I was through with him. He had been my doctor for over 20 years.

People have asked why I did not sue him. What was most important to me was getting well; I focused all of my energy and concentration on that.

Each day I would walk a little more, and then I would rest and walk a little more. I was still weak but my spirits were high.

Tim and I settled into a routine, up at 5:00 on Tuesday, Thursday and Saturday and then off to dialysis. During my treatment he would go to have breakfast and then to Home Depot. This became his routine. He did not want to stay at the dialysis center; however, he did not want to be too far away.

Tim would get frustrated because I still would not eat much. I tried protein drinks; they usually came back up as soon as they hit my stomach. Till this day, I cannot handle the taste of protein drinks or supplements.

In August, Tim's nephew Keith was getting married, in Southern California. I knew Tim really wanted to attend this wedding. All of his brothers and sisters were going to be there. He felt there was no way we could attend. The wedding was early on a Saturday evening and I had dialysis that day. He called his brother, David, and let him know we would not be able to attend.

A couple of days before the wedding I asked Tim if he wanted to go to the wedding and he said "How can we?" "You have dialysis on that day." I told him we could leave after dialysis and drive down to Ventura, we may not make it in time for the ceremony but we would be there for the reception. He asked if I thought I would be up to the trip. I told him there should not be a problem; I could always sleep in the car. He said I needed to ask the doctor. I smiled and said, "I already have." She told me that I could go as long as we made several stops so I could stretch my legs.

On Saturday, after dialysis, we left for Ventura. The trip was 370 miles and would take about six hours to get there. We stopped a few times so I could stretch my legs. I was able to rest and get some sleep while Tim was driving. We reached our destination around 5:00 PM. We checked into our hotel which was next to where the wedding was going to be held. We changed clothes and were able to make it to the wedding before the ceremony started.

The wedding was outdoors at a county club. The setting was beautiful. It was great to see all of Tim's brothers and sisters and their spouses.

Before the reception even began, I started to get tired. After about 30 minutes I asked Tim if he could take me back to the hotel because I needed to rest. When we got to our room I told him to go back to the reception and I would call him when I was ready to come back over. He did not want to leave me alone but I convinced him I would be alright, and I was.

I called Tim about 90 minutes later and asked him to come back and get me. He and our nephew, Alex came to pick me up. We stayed there for about an hour and I was ready to leave. This time Tim said he was ready to call it a night.

The next morning we met Tim's family for breakfast. It was there that Tim's sister; Gail told me that when I was healthy enough for a kidney transplant she would give me one of her kidneys. I was astounded. I could not believe anyone would offer to donate a kidney to me. I asked her if she was sure. She said, "Absolutely, I only need one." The feeling that came over me was indescribable. It would be three and a half years later before the transplant would come to be.

Tim grew up in Oxnard, CA, after breakfast he took me around the area to show me some of the sights. The beaches were so beautiful, it took my breath away. In my opinion there were no beaches in Northern California that could compare. I asked him how he could leave this area. He said, "I had to come find you."

He took me to one beach in particular that had a pier. He took the wheel chair out of the back of the car and away we went. Only one problem, one of the front wheels kept falling off. Tim would put it back on; we would go a little further and it would fall off again. Every time the wheel came off we would just laugh and laugh. We decided to turn around and when the wheel fell off again, I told him I would walk the rest of the way.

Later that afternoon everyone went to David and his wife Carol's home for a BBQ. To everyone's delight Gail made her famous cinnamon nut rolls. She made a small pan without the nuts just for me because I was not allowed to have them on my dialysis diet.

We went back to the hotel in the early evening, watched a movie and Tim packed the suitcase for our return home on Monday.

It was a wonderful trip. Tim had the opportunity to visit with all of his brothers and sisters, their spouses and many of his nieces and nephews. We were both happy we had made the trip.

Tuesday we were back to the same routine. Tuesday, Thursday and Saturday to dialysis and whatever I felt up to on the other days.

Tim began working on a pond for the backyard in late August. This helped him keep his sanity during all of this madness called my recovery.

Dr. Shea, an associate of Dr. Rae told me it was time to meet with the transplant teams at UC Davis, UCSF and Las Vegas and get on the kidney transplant waiting list. He said that I needed to get put on a list so that clock would start and time would begin to elapse.

Each hospital had a different average length of time that it would take for a kidney to become available; UC Davis was three to four years, UCSF was seven plus and Sunrise Hospital in Las Vegas was two years.

I contacted UC Davis and set up the appointment on the Friday before Labor Day. My appointment at UC Davis was a disaster. It was in Sacramento on a Friday afternoon prior to a holiday weekend. The traffic was unbearable! I met with their team; a social worker and a nurse who both asked me a lot of questions but were very positive. The doctor came in took one look at me without introducing herself and said, "You will never be eligible to have a kidney transplant." Imagine my shock and bewilderment. I knew that I still had additional weight to lose, but I had already lost more than 100 pounds. My thoughts, "Bet Me!" Then she told me that they would not add me to their list and that I would get a denial letter in the mail.

My appointment with the UCSF transplant team would not happen until April, 2008.

In September, Dr. Shea came to see me at the dialysis center and said it was time to get a fistula. This is a vein that is grown in my arm and once developed it would be used for my dialysis instead of the catheter that was in my chest. Dr. Shea indicated using the fistula would allow the dialysis machine to clean my blood more thoroughly. He also said once the vein is working properly, they would take out the catheter and within a week I should be able to take a shower!

Dr. Shea referred me to Dr. Otero, a General Surgeon, in Pleasant Hill, California. He said there would be a wait to see him, but he was worth the wait because he was the best. It took a month to get the appointment.

My appointment with Dr. Otero was the first week of November. He said they would do the surgery in two weeks and it would take about six weeks to develop. If the surgery was a success, I would be able to take that shower around the first of the year!

In early December I told Tim that I was thinking of going back to work. He said he preferred that I wait until the spring. That was fine with me.

The timeframe for returning to work was made for me when I received a letter later that week from my employer indicating that if I did not return to work before December 31, 2007, my medical insurance would be terminated. I called my doctor's office and told them I would like to return to work. Dr. Rae said since I had a home office she would sign the release for me to return to work.

I sent an email to my new supervisor, Shelby Bennett, and let her know I would be coming back to work in two weeks. She was thrilled that I was able to return. We talked on the phone and she told me that on dialysis days if I felt tired, I should rest. She knew that my work assignments would always be on time. I prepared to return to work in ten days.

Each year Tim and I have a holiday open house. Most people who attend only see each other at this event and the annual BBQ we normally have each summer. It is a good time for everyone to catch up on each other's lives. This year was particularly interesting because I was so weak during the summer we were unable to have the BBQ. Many of our friends had not seen me in a long time either and were surprised to see how much weight I had lost. Everyone ate and got caught up on the trials and the tribulations of the past year. As always it was great to get together with our friends. We wished them all Happy Holidays and they were on their way.

The next day I would start working again.

Shelby made returning to work a smooth transition. She insisted that I rest when I was tired. I made sure that all of my assignments were turned in on time. The holidays came and went without much fanfare. The family came over to our home, as was traditional. Tim and I cooked dinner the usual - spaghetti and meatballs, it had become a family tradition years ago. Everyone opened their presents and commented how strange it was without now my Mom as well as my Dad and Jim.

On New Year's Eve, Tim and I spent a quiet evening at home and looked forward to the New Year.

CHAPTER 4

To sum up my first six months since being diagnosed with end stage renal disease (kidney failure), I was stronger, could walk without getting out of breath and able to do most things for myself. I no longer need to have Tim's help when bathing. I was able to drive again. I had lost over 120 pounds and was feeling much better.

The first week of January, 2008, Dr. Otero said that my fistula had developed and I was ready to have them start using it during my next dialysis. I asked him how long it would take before I could use the shower. He told me that I needed to give it a week and if all went well, they would take out the catheter and I could then use the shower. The next week, Dr. Shea came into the dialysis center and told me to come by the office after dialysis and he would remove the catheter.

Joy took me to Dr. Shea's office and all he had to do was make a small incision, give it a little tug and the catheter came out. He said I needed to wait three days before I could take my shower.

On Sunday morning, I stepped in the shower; just having the water run over my body was an incredible feeling. It had been nearly six months since the last time I was in a shower. I am a person who takes a shower every day, so it was very difficult having had that restriction. Tim kept coming in to check on me. He said he thought I was never going to come out.

Tim found a temporary position as a mortgage underwriter in February. His job was not far from where I had dialysis. He would drop me off on his way to work and Joy would pick me up. This went on a couple of months and then I told them it was time for me to start taking myself.

Going through dialysis can take a toll on your body and sometimes your mental health. Here is what a typical day at dialysis was for me. I would get up at 4:45 AM; three days a week and drive to the dialysis clinic. My dialysis began at 5:45 AM. I would go into the room and weigh in (this would tell them how much fluid I had gained since the prior dialysis treatment – fluid was to be kept to a minimum at all times.) Next I would go to my recliner (everyone usually had the same spot each time.) The tech would put my legs up and put the blood pressure cuff on my arm (this would remain on my arm the entire treatment – blood pressure readings were taken often.) The tech would then insert two needles into my fistula (one to pull the blood out so the machine could clean my blood and pull the excess fluid out – the other to return my blood.) My temperature was taken both before and after my treatment. The nurse would come over and take my vitals. My arm had to remain completely still during the dialysis. There was no getting up because I was hooked up to the machine. I would then sit for three hours while the machine acted as my artificial kidney.

During the long three hours I would try to sleep. If I could sleep the time seemed to pass by faster. If I could not sleep I would read a book. I got through a lot of books in my time there. Sometimes I would just look around see what everyone else was doing. The techs and the nurse would come by and visit, that was always a fun time.

Dialysis is much harder than people who have not experienced it may think. I have had people ask me, "How can you do that week after week?" I would tell them, nobody wakes up in the morning and says "Wow, I get to go to dialysis today," but it is saving my life and many others' as well.

I recently heard there are over 500,000 dialysis patients in the United States. That number is growing daily. It is now said that over 80% of the population either has a family member or knows of someone that is on dialysis.

However difficult this procedure is, it extends numerous lives every year. I was fortunate to have a family member give me one of her kidneys. Some are given a kidney because they were at the top of the list and a kidney has become available. There are others who have chosen not to have a transplant for their own personal reasons. Some simply are not eligible (they may have health problems that prevent the transplant and others may have a weight problem) and then there are those who did not make it.

In April of 2008, I met with a transplant coordinator and a doctor at UCSF. They told me that although I was not eligible for a transplant at that time they would put my name on the transplant list as inactive so the clock would start and time would begin to elapse. Not long after my appointment with UCSF I received a letter from Sunrise Hospital in Las Vegas saying they were sorry but they were closing their transplant unit.

In 2008 several patients at the dialysis clinic died. There were six that passed away on the days that I went. The saddest for me was my friend, Aileen. She had several problems with her heart and her blood pressure would drop every time she had a treatment. I felt so bad for her. On the Saturday before she passed away, she told me, "Linda, I cannot do this anymore." I tried to comfort her and tell her she was going to be alright, but in my heart I knew she was not. On Tuesday morning, we were told that she had died on Sunday. It was a very difficult morning for me. Chuck (Aileen's husband) came by to see me, and he told me what had happened. My heart went out to him.

In April, Shelby, my supervisor at work, was diagnosed with bladder cancer and died in August. It was so sad for all of us who worked for her. She was such a pleasure to work with.

Earlier in the year, a friend of mine, Maryann Evans, saw me at a local restaurant and said the doctors told her she may have to go dialysis soon. She said this frightened her. I spent some time with her explaining how dialysis worked, and reassuring her that she would be alright if this came to pass. A month later she told me she would be starting dialysis. Her daughter offered to give her one of her kidneys, but she declined. She did not want her daughter to take the risk. Maryann had decided she would prefer to have dialysis done at home rather than go into the clinic. She wanted the freedom to be able to travel. There are many patients that do this. She started the training and was told there was a procedure that needed to be done prior to having the port placed in her body. They wanted to make sure the vein in her neck was clear. While she was in the hospital something happened and she passed away. Hers would be the fourth funeral I had attended that year, all who had been on dialysis. There was still one more to come and that was Shelby's Memorial Service in August.

It was an emotional rollercoaster. I was feeling as well as could be expected for someone that was on dialysis, but seeing so many people die makes you think about your own mortality.

I decided it was time to bring Jeff Levy back into my life. He was my grief counselor when my brother died in 2000 and helped me through a number of things through the years. He now has a thriving practice in North Carolina. We have been doing sessions over the phone for a number of years. I cannot tell you how much he has gotten me through. What a blessing to have him in my life.

In August, 2008, I told Tim that I wanted to start taking swimming lessons. He thought that was a strange idea since I was afraid to put my face in the water. I told him I loved the water and maybe someone could find the magic that would make it possible for me to swim. As always he was supportive and said I should go for it.

I found a place in El Sobrante, Canyon Swim School, which primarily was for children, but they did have a few adult classes. Joy decided that she would take them with me. We took the classes on Mondays and Wednesday (non-dialysis days).

The third week of the class I developed an eye infection. The infection lingered on until the following February. It was so bad that I had to wear sunglasses all the time. Any type of light would hurt my eyes. The eye doctor told me it was a virus that was going around and was so contagious that it could very easily go into my other eye. It went back and forth between both eyes for several months.

Because of the eye infection, we had to go back to the routine of Tim taking me to dialysis in the morning and Joy picking me up. The lights from oncoming cars would hurt my eyes to the point I would have to close them, so I could not drive.

In September, Tim and I went back to Pennsylvania for a family reunion on my Mom's side of the family, the Pia's. I set up my dialysis in New Castle and treatments continued just as they had at home; Tuesday and Thursday, but since the reunion was on Saturday and not knowing how I would feel after dialysis, I set my Saturday's appointment up for the following Monday.

We stayed with my cousin Sam and his wife Patty. Sam is my Dad's brother's son. They set up a mini family reunion with the Allen side. I got to see and spend time with my cousins Elaine and her husband Joe, Michael and his wife Laurie, and Sam's brother Larry. I had not seen some of these family members in over 30 years. It was a fun time had by all.

The next day, after dialysis, Sam and Patty took us for a ride; we were on our way to the Seneca Casino and Hotel in Allegany near the New York border. Patty had made reservations for us to spend the night. The countryside as well as the hotel was beautiful. My eye infection reappeared when we arrived at the casino. The lights hurt my eyes. I spent the evening in our room. I had brought all of my medication with me just in case. After a few hours it settled down and I could go downstairs as long as I did not look directly at any of the lights. We had a great time in spite of the eye infection.

We went to the family reunion and there must have been over 60 family members attending. Most everyone lived in the area with the exception of Tim and I, my Aunt Patty and my cousin, Marsha, live in Northern California and my cousin Sondra and her husband Rick live near Hershey, Pennsylvania. We had never seen so much food. It appeared that everyone made their favorites and brought enough for 60 people or more. Sondra had made several different kinds of Italian cookies. In addition there were hotdogs and hamburgers cooking on the grill. There were three of my aunts at the reunion. In addition to Aunt Patty, there was Aunt Julia and Aunt Mary who has since passed away; all three widows of my Mom's brothers. There were so many cousins and their children that I could not begin to name them all. Some I had met and others that were new introductions. It was such a great trip.

I was not looking forward to returning to work. Things had changed drastically. My new supervisor was a micro-manager. She wanted to know what I was doing every minute of the day. There was no time given to me to rest. I had been with the company for nine years and never with this type of management. The stress was beginning to mount. I was tired all the time.

In January of 2009, the company changed the way it handled Family Leave. I was told I had to report every hour I was off to this company. It became very cumbersome. I later found out that since I was an exempt employee there was no need to report these times. For the first time in all the years I had been with the company I was not happy. But I was stuck! Who was going to hire someone that had to be out two partial mornings a week, and besides I had to have medical insurance.

It looked like Tim was going to be hired as a permanent employee where he had been a temp for nearly a year. If this happened we would be able to have medical benefits through his company. Seeing the stress that I was under, he said that as soon as he was hired as a permanent employee he wanted me to see if the doctor would put me on disability for a while to ease the stress. He became permanent effective the first of February and benefits would begin that day.

I had decided that I wanted to change dialysis centers to be closer to home. I called the El Cerrito clinic and was told they did have openings; however I would need to meet with the doctor for an evaluation and she would make the final decision.

I met with the doctor and during the examination I asked her if I could go on disability for a month, maybe two. She replied "Don't you know dialysis is a full-time job?" She did the evaluation and approved my transferring to her clinic and indicated she was going to write up the report to say a minimum of three months on disability was required.

I had asked if it was possible to have my dialysis on Monday, Wednesday and Friday. This way I would have the weekends off to spend with Tim. Not only were they able to get me on those days they were also able to get me scheduled on the first shift.

My disability was to start on January 30, 2009.

CHAPTER 5

Three days prior to my starting in El Cerrito, I met with the social worker, Susan. I learned more from her in one hour than I had learned the entire time I was in Concord. She advised me to sign up for Social Security Disability. She said it took about four months to get approved. Patients with end stage renal disease were almost always approved. I told her that I was not planning on going on permanent disability. She told me it never hurts to have it approved. She was right! It took about four months and much to my surprise I went on Social Security Disability the month after approval.

The dialysis center was an older one, not new like the one I had just left. However, I felt the care was better. My nurse was Leah and my tech, Norman. They were terrific. I was so happy I had made the change.

The early morning patients became a very close knit group. There was never a dull moment. It was a group that supported each other. If someone was down, the rest of the group would pick them up. If someone was not there, everyone got concerned.

Not having to work took a lot of stress off of me. I was able to get the rest my body so desperately needed at the time.

It was in April, 2009, that I started my swimming lessons again. I called Canyon Pool and since my dialysis was now on Monday, Wednesday and Friday, I scheduled my classes for Tuesday and Thursday night. This time Joy had decided not to join.

I went to the class and was assigned to a different instructor, his name was Joe Perelli. There was one other lady in the class. He asked what our experience level was. I told Joe I was a beginner's, beginner. I explained how I had started lessons the previous year and what had happened. I was still apprehensive about putting my face in the water. He told me not to worry that before the session was over I would not be afraid anymore. He was very patient. I was learning a little more each class. I really looked forward to Tuesday and Thursday nights.

One day the other lady was not there and I got the feel for what it was like to have private lessons. The next session I took private lessons and the one after that as well. By the end of the spring session I was no longer afraid to put my face in the water. I could actually swim. Not great, but I could swim.

I had explained to Joe that my optimal goal was to get in good enough condition to have a kidney transplant. I told him I had to lose more weight and thought the swimming would help towards that goal.

Joe told me that he would be switching from teaching at night to teaching days during the summer and the classes were four days a week. I wanted to stay working with him but how could I when I had dialysis on Monday and Wednesday? I decided to go to the YMCA (I was a member there at the time) on a dialysis day just to see if I could do it. I put a waterproof bandage over the needle holes in my arms and off I went to see if the bandage would keep water out. It did. I was thrilled. Now I could do the summer sessions.

My private classes were set up in the early afternoon so that I would have time to rest after my dialysis.

I looked forward to my classes and usually went early to watch the children swim. They ranged from babies to their teens. It was so much fun. They had classes every 30 minutes starting at 9:00 in the morning until 7:30 at night. Most classes were full with a waiting list. They had been around so long that my adult nieces and my nephew took classes there when they were in daycare.

My swimming improved with each session. You would never know that just a few months earlier I was afraid to put my face in the water. Joe was such a good teacher.

I would try and swim a couple of other days a week at the YMCA, but there never seemed to be any lanes available. I was getting frustrated by this and the final straw for me was the day a lady came to share my lane. Her joining me was not the problem; she got in the middle of the lane and just stayed there. I did not want to get into an argument with an elderly lady so I decided it was time for a change.

The next day I asked Joe where he went swimming. He said that he belonged to Lakeridge Athletic Club in El Sobrante. I went there the next day to check it out. As it turned out they had a summer membership special going on. I saw the pool and that was all I needed. I became a member that day and signed up for the next year. I am still a member there today.

I found the club to be friendly. People were all shapes, sizes and ages. There was no staring at people who did not look like them; like I had witnessed at other places. It was sad for me when the summer sessions ended because the swim school would be closed until the following spring. I had learned a lot but I still had so far to go. I was going to miss the staff and the routine.

I talked to Joe and he agreed to work with me for a while. That while lasted until the swim school opened again in the spring. We would meet at Lakeridge a few days a week after he got off work. We swam rain or shine. The club pool has an outdoor pool.

We started out in the shallow area of the pool since that is what I had been used to. He worked me hard on days that I did not have dialysis and knew just how far to push me when I did. My swimming improved every week.

One afternoon Joe said it was time to go into the lanes. I was not sure I was ready for this. The lane at the deep end went to 12 feet. The deepest I had ever gone was 5 feet. The first week we went only to about 6 feet.

At the end of the first week, Joe said he thought it was time for me to get goggles and fins. He knew a place in Concord. I met him there and he recommended a pair of Spiedo goggles that fit just perfect and then he chose the fins he thought would work best for me.

After a week with my new goggles and my new fins, Joe told me it was time for me to swim the length of the pool. I asked if he really thought I was ready for this. He told me that if he did not think I was ready he would not have encouraged me.

I made my way to the other end of the pool, but was not quite sure how I was to turn around and come back. I did what I could, but awkward as it was, I made it back, safe and sound. After watching me struggle for a few days, Joe said I was making him nervous with my "turnaround technique". Joe showed me a technique that worked much better. Now the return trip in the lane was much smoother.

Swimming had become a passion in my life. I was swimming six, sometimes seven days a week. My lap count started to climb, 10, 20, 30 and by the end of November I was up to 50 laps on non-dialysis days and 40 on days when I had a treatment. It gave me something to look forward to every day. I loved every minute of it and I was helping myself get stronger.

I remember one day at Lakeridge, I had just finished swimming, and a man came up to me that I don't remember seeing. He said that he had been watching me swim over the months and was impressed at how much I had improved. I thanked him for noticing. He then said that I was a real inspiration. I thanked him again. I thought to myself; imagine me being an inspiration to someone. This was not the last time someone would say this to me.

Swimming was my salvation. No matter how I was feeling, especially on dialysis days, when I finished my laps I always felt much better. My ultimate goal was to get into good enough shape to be able to have that kidney transplant.

In October, Tim and I went to Disneyworld in Florida. I mention this to show that although a person is on dialysis they can still travel. All I had to do to get my dialysis set was to call a hotline number that the clinic had, tell them where I was going and they would set up my appointments. There are even a few cruise lines that offer dialysis on board. Prior to arriving at Disneyworld, I rented a scooter that would be delivered to the hotel where we were staying and I would have use of it the entire time we were there. This made the trip more enjoyable because I never would have been able to walk through the parks. Disneyworld's transportation busses accommodated the scooter, so there were no issues getting to the parks.

Dialysis continued three days a week. Some days were good and others not so good. There were days I could go out and do things after dialysis and others when all I did was rest until it was time to go swimming. The worst days were when my blood pressure would drop. When this happened, I would get light headed and just feel really bad. The tech would have to stop the machine from taking fluid. They would lay my head back and wait for me to start feeling better. There were times when I would get leg cramps. My new tech, Nita, would say to me "Just push hard with your foot on my hip, I can take it," then she would give me some fluid back. In a few minutes, that seemed more like an hour, the cramps would finally stop. These are just some of the side effects of dialysis.

With the procedure itself, and the high and low blood pressure that goes along with it, dialysis can be very hard on your heart.

CHAPTER 6

My weight had been stable for about a year. I had lost 190 pounds and my body seemed to say no more. Even with all the swimming I could not get past this plateau. I knew that in order to have the kidney transplant, I would have to lose about another 40 pounds.

I left a message for my Transplant Coordinator at UCSF the last week of October, 2009. I wanted to discuss what options I might have to get the rest of the weight off. I did not hear back from her. In the past, sometimes it would take three or four weeks before she would get back to me. Not once in all the times that I called her did she ever answer the phone.

The first week in December I told Tim that I was calling Stanford Hospital and Clinics to see if I could meet with their transplant team. He said, "Go for it."

I made the call and told the operator I would like to make an appointment to meet with their kidney transplant team. She transferred me the kidney transplant department. I explained to the person on the telephone that I would like to make an appointment to meet with the kidney transplant team. She asked who was referring me. I told her I was referring myself. She said that was fine and asked for my insurance information. She told me someone would call me when they received the approval from the insurance company, which would take about two weeks.

Sure enough Patty Francois, from the transplant department called me in two weeks to tell me the insurance approved the visit, and she could now set up the appointment for me.

She said that I needed to make two different appointments; one for an educational class and the other was to meet with the transplant team. I asked her if there was any way I could do it all in one day because I lived over an hour away. Patty said she would do that for me.

My first appointment with the Stanford Transplant Team was set for December 23, 2009. She told me that they encouraged patients to bring advocates with them. I thanked her.

First, I called Tim to let him know the appointment was set up. He said he was unable to go with me. Next I called my friend Dar and asked her if she wanted to go. She said of course and that Dave could drive us because he closes the shop the last two weeks of the year.

I was so excited, I was going to Stanford!

CHAPTER
7

On the morning of December 23, 2009, Dave and Dar picked me up at 6:00 AM and we were on our way to Stanford. My first appointment was at 8:00 AM and I was told the educational class would last about three hours and I would meet with the transplant team from 1:00 pm until 5:00 PM.

When I signed in for the class for information on kidney transplants, I was given a folder with my name on it. Inside the folder there were a lot of information and lab slips. I had never received anything like this from the other hospitals. The class was very informative. I asked a few questions, but mostly just took it all in.

The class lasted about two hours. I was then told to go and have my blood drawn, get a chest x-ray and an EKG. I had 13 tubes of blood taken (they wanted 14 but my vein said no more). I was also told to come back in the afternoon to have four more tubes drawn. I had the x-ray and the EKG. Everything took less than an hour. We had lunch in the cafeteria; we had about 90 minutes before my appointment with the transplant team.

We arrived at the clinic at 12:45 PM and I was taken in right then to have my weight and my vitals taken. One of the assistants took me into a room and told me to have a seat on the chair next to the computer. He told me the nurse would be in soon and he went to get Dave and Dar.

The nurse came in and asked several questions and then told me that she didn't think there was anything they could do for me because of my weight. Then she said "But, we are doing a study with dialysis patients that have gastric bypass surgery." I told her I was not interested in having gastric bypass surgery. She again told me that she did not think they could do anything for me. She left and told me the fellow would be in next.

I did not know at the time what a fellow (a medical doctor on a fellowship who wanted to specialize in a specific area) was. She came in and asked me several questions (most were the same questions the nurse asked). Then she repeated the same thing as the nurse. She did not think there was anything they could do for me because of my weight and then told me about the study. I told her I was not interested in having the gastric bypass surgery. She said she wanted to examine me. While she was examining me, she brought up the study once again. I told her that I had already expressed my feelings to her about the study. I asked her if they would consider any of the extra skin I have when determining how much weight I needed to lose to be eligible for the transplant surgery. She said, "Oh you only have about five pounds of extra skin." I told her I had five pounds of extra skin where you shouldn't have extra skin. As she left the room she once again told me she did not think they could do anything for me. I looked at Dave and Dar and I said "This isn't looking very good."

About 10 minutes later in walked Dr. John Scandling and the fellow. He introduced himself, handed me his card and said "You must be so frustrated." He had me there. He said that I should be very proud of myself for what I had accomplished. At that time I had lost a total of 190 pounds and was swimming 40 laps six days a week. He explained to me why I needed to lose the additional weight. I told him I understood that, but that my body just stopped giving up the weight. He said that I could have bariatric surgery. I told him I was not having gastric bypass surgery. He told me there were other options. I told him I would consider the lap band. I asked him the same question about the extra skin and he indicated that no one had ever asked them that question before. He then asked me to lie down on the examining table. He pushed down on my sides and was surprised that he could feel my hip bones. He said "You do have a lot of extra skin". He then told me that he could not make that decision, only the transplant surgeon could make that call. He told me that he would speak to Dr. Marc Melcher and see if he would be willing to see me. He told me that the transplant surgeons typically do not meet with kidney transplant patients until closer to the transplant date.

He gave me Dr. Melcher's card and Dr. Morton's card (the director of bariatric program).

He said the transplant team meets every Tuesday to talk about the new cases that came in since their meeting the prior week. I asked him about being put on their transplant list as inactive as UCSF had. He said they do not put anyone on the waiting list on an inactive status. He told me that someone would call me and let me know the results of their meeting.

When Dr. Scandling left, I looked at his card and was amazed to see that he was the Professor of Medicine and the Medical Director of Kidney and Pancreas Transplantation.

Next person to come in was the social worker, Selly Castillo. What a breath of fresh air! She was so positive about everything and told me she would be with me throughout the life of my new kidney. She gave me her card and told me to call her at any time if I needed anything.

When we were on our way home from Stanford, we all felt cautiously optimistic and very impressed with Dr. Scandling and Selly.

True to their word, I received a call the following Wednesday. The person told me she was calling me because my nurse coordinator was on vacation. (I didn't know I even had a nurse coordinator.) She told me that they were holding their decision about putting me on their transplant list pending my visit with the transplant surgeon. She said that Dr. Melcher's scheduler was on vacation and she would call me on Monday to set up an appointment. I was told that he only scheduled appointments on Tuesday afternoons. I thanked her. I was so excited that he had agreed to see me!

I figured that since he only had appointments once a week, it was going to be awhile before I would be able to see him. But that was okay because the fact that he was going to see me was more than I had hoped for.

I called Tim at work and to let him know about the call I received from Stanford. He said he wanted to come to that appointment. Then I called Dar and she said she wanted to come too.

The following Monday morning I received a call from Dr. Melcher's office and they set the appointment for the 19th of January. I was so amazed!

Tuesday morning, January 19, 2010 around 11:00 AM, Tim, Dar, Paula Land (another friend of mine) and I headed for Stanford for my first appointment with Dr. Melcher. I remember being both excited and apprehensive. It would be up to him if I had the opportunity to move forward towards a kidney transplant with Stanford. Everyone was looking forward to meeting Dr. Melcher.

At 1:00 PM, they took us into the examination room. We had been sitting there a few minutes and in walked the fellow, Dr. Amy Gallo. The first thing she said to me was, "We are going to get this done!" She congratulated me on all that I had accomplished. She asked a few questions and told me she wanted to examine me. She asked Tim, Dar and Paula if they wanted to stay. They all said "no" and headed for the waiting room.

As she was examining me we talked. I explained to her why I did not want to have a gastric bypass surgery. She understood my reasons. I told her I knew that I still had additional weight to lose and was considering the lap band. She told me that Dr. Melcher would discuss my options when he came in. She told me she knew he was going to want me to lose more weight before he would perform the surgery. Our conversation was pleasant and I liked her a lot. She told me she was going to get Dr. Melcher and they would be back soon. When she left the room I was beginning to feel hopeful.

When Dr. Melcher walked in, my first impression was how young he was. He came over to me and introduced himself and then said "Tell me your story." "Tell me how you went from someone who weighed 446 pounds who could not walk across a room without getting out of breath to 256 pounds and swims 40 laps six or seven days a week."

So, I told him my story. I told him how the doctor in Las Vegas said I did not have a long life expectancy, that I was going to have stroke after stroke after stroke and I was going to die. That my reaction to that was "No I'm not, you just figured out what was wrong with me." I knew that once that was figured out I was going to be okay. That I knew it was going to be a long recovery period but that I would make it.

As far as the swimming, I started out afraid to put my face in the water and had a great teacher that got me to the point I was now. I told him swimming had become a passion of mine. I am not sure if I told him or not, the pool I swim in is 75 feet in length and goes up to 12' deep.

He told me he had never met anyone that accomplished what I had. What a compliment!

He examined me and said that I would need to lose some more weight and the reasons why. We then talked about my options for losing weight. We both knew that gastric bypass was out. I told him I would consider the lap band. He explained he did not want anything foreign put into my body. So I asked, since the gastric bypass is out and the lap band is out, what are our options? He went over all of the options and he said he thought the sleeve gastrectomy was best one for me. I told him I had never heard of that, and asked what it was all about. He told me the doctor would block off 75% of my stomach and it would be the shape of half of a banana, and there were no side effects like those with the gastric bypass. He went on to say that with all surgeries there were risks. I told him the benefits would outweigh the risks. Then I asked him what was next.

Dr. Melcher indicated that the best doctor to perform the surgery for me was Dr. Lau. I mentioned that Dr. Scandling had indicated another doctor, but he said "Dr. Lau is for you." Dr. Gallo readily agreed. She told me I would really like him.

Dr. Melcher said that he shared the clinic with Dr. Lau on Thursday and would refer me to him then. Dr. Melcher told me that I should receive a call from Dr. Lau's scheduler soon after.

He asked me if I would like to be part of a study they were doing for dialysis patients that had bariatric surgery. I told him sure, that would be no problem. He explained a month after I had the surgery they would be able to put me on the transplant list.

I advised him that I had two possible donors; my sister-in-law Gail, who lives in Indiana and my friend Carol Carter who lives in Las Vegas. He said that there were advantages to having a living donor. At the end of our appointment, both he and Dr. Gallo wished me well and said they would see me again. I really liked both of these doctors!

When I walked into the waiting room there sat Tim, Dar and Paula; they never got to meet Dr. Melcher that day. I asked them what happened, how come they never came back in. They told me no one ever came back to get them.

On our way home I told everyone how well the appointment went and that I had decided to have the sleeve gastrectomy. When I told them what it was, they were all a little surprised because no one had heard of this before. I explained to them what Dr. Melcher had told me and everyone thought it was a good idea. I was so excited when I left there because I thought things were really starting to move forward. Now all I had to do was to wait for the call from Dr. Lau's scheduler. Thankfully, I did not have to wait long for his office to call. It came two days later. Jovie, from Dr. Lau's office called me to schedule my appointment for the following Friday. Once again I called Dar and asked her if she wanted to go with me. She said "count me in."

The week seemed to fly by. Dar picked me up after my dialysis and we took off for Stanford. When we arrived, they took us right in. The assistant said that the fellow would be in shortly.

When the fellow came in he started asking a lot of questions that really did not pertain to me, but he was following a script. I told him I wanted to get this done as soon as possible. He told me there were certain things that had to be done prior to the surgery. I told him, "Look I already lost 190 pounds do I really have to do all of these things?" He said he would ask Dr. Lau. He had that look on his face that said he really did not want to ask him. He left the room and about ten minutes later Dr. Lau came in.

His first words to me were "*I am Jim Lau and there will be no short cuts!*" My first thoughts were Dr. Gallo thought I was really going to like this doctor? He went on to explain about the requirements that had to be completed before surgery could happen; different tests and classes that I would need to attend. I knew it wasn't going to happen anytime soon because the one class that was mandatory happened only once a month and that class was held two days prior to my appointment. He went on to explain what was involved by having the sleeve gastrectomy. How they would remove 75% of my stomach (Dar told me later she thought I was going to slide off the chair when he told me that) and what is left looks like a half of a banana. He said there was not a lot of long-term documentation on this since it had not been around as long as the other bariatric surgeries. I asked him how soon we could have the sleeve done.

Dr. Lau said the insurance companies had some requirements before they would approve the surgery. I had to attend a mandatory class on bariatric surgeries, meet with a psychiatrist, a nutritionist and have a few medical procedures. He said there was one procedure, called an EGD (endoscopic gastro duodenoscopy) a scope is put inside of my stomach to make sure there were no problems going on inside. He said he could do that one there at Stanford if I preferred. I told him that would be my preference since he would be doing the surgery.

Dr. Lau went on and spoke about a few other things and looked like he was getting ready to leave the room and then he asked if I had any questions. I told him just one. I asked "How soon after surgery can I go back to swimming?" He had this strange look on his face that said to me, nobody ever asks me about exercise and then sat back in his chair. It was like a totally different doctor had come in the room. He was nice as could be. This was probably the person Dr. Gallo had talked about. We talked for a while longer and became buddies after that. I asked him how soon we could get this done. He told me he was about three months out, but he could get me in sooner if all of the pre-op requirements were completed. He walked me out to the receptionist desk and this is where I met the bariatric nurse coordinator, Michael Torno. He gave me all of the paperwork I needed to get started and set up my appointment for the test Dr. Lau was going to do. I would end up depending a lot on Michael.

A new journey was about to begin.

CHAPTER 8

All of my appointments were set up. Tim and I decided that since the procedure that Dr. Lau had to do was on the same day of the mandatory meeting we would just spend the day in the Stanford are

I received a call from my insurance carrier and they indicated that they had a partnership with Tim's employer and Stanford so getting the approval through was going to be easy. Susan said she would be my coordinator and would approve the surgery within two to three days after she received all of the paperwork from Stanford. She also gave me the name of the psychologist they wanted me to see.

The first thing on the agenda was to have the procedure done in the hospital. Things went just as smooth as Dr. Lau had indicated.

Next came the mandatory meeting. I was surprised how many people were there. My guess would be between 75 and 80.

The first person to speak was a nutritionist. She started out talking about the bariatric program. Then she talked about the required foods and supplements. She said there were calcium supplements and other items that I knew would not work for a person on dialysis. I raised my hand, I was ignored. She continued to talk, I said "Excuse me," again I was ignored. Then I said "I have a question." She looked at me like she was annoyed that I had a question. I told her that as a dialysis patient I had to watch my calcium intake and she said in an irritated voice, "You mean phosphorus" and totally dismissed me. Instead of making a scene, I decided that I would deal with her in the meeting I had scheduled with her the following week. I spoke with Dr. Lau after the meeting and he said, "Don't worry, he and I would figure out what I should eat."

When Dar and I arrived at the appointment with the nutritionist, she started with the same story. Again I told her I had to watch my calcium intake. She told me she was previously a dialysis nutritionist and she knew what she was talking about. I then told her that I had been a dialysis patient for the past two and a half years and I knew what I could and couldn't have. She then went to the computer and looked something up. Then she told me it would be best if I talked with the nutritionist at the dialysis center. She went on to say a few more things. At this point I wasn't even listening to her.

The next day I went and talked with Caley, the nutritionist at the dialysis center and told her all about my visit. She told me that she would develop a food program that would fit into what they were looking for at Stanford and that would also work for me. Caley had the diet plan ready the following week.

A couple of weeks later I had my appointment with a psychiatrist in Berkeley, California. This was an interesting visit. We spoke for about 30 minutes. She told me that the insurance company required that I take a test. The test was 252 questions, several which were repeats of previous questions. The psychiatrist told me that she would have the results of the test in about a week, and then she would forward it to the insurance company. This now completed all of my pre-op requirements. All that was left was for Stanford to receive the approval from the insurance company and the surgery to be scheduled.

After a few obstacles at Dr. Lau's office, which were taken care of by Michael, Dr. Lau and with the help of Dr. Melcher, the surgery was approved by the insurance company and scheduled for April 8, 2010. I was so excited!

I received an email from Dr. Lau indicating he was sorry, but due to a conflict he needed to reschedule my surgery for April 6. Can you imagine an email from the doctor rather than a call from his assistant? I was impressed.

I had two appointments scheduled prior to surgery. One was a group meeting with the nutritionist combined with the nurse coordinator, Michael, on Thursday and the other was with Dr. Lau on Friday.

Two days before I was to meet with Dr. Lau, when I came home from swimming I had a message from Dr. Melcher asking me to call him. When I returned his call, he asked if I still wanted to take part in the study. I told him I would. He told he would have the forms sent out that day and told me it was important that I sign and return them as soon as possible. I told him about my appointment with Dr. Lau and asked him if he would like for me to come by his office and sign the papers at that time. He told me that would be a good idea.

I told Dr. Melcher about the issues I had with the nutritionist. I explained to him I felt they needed someone who understood the needs of dialysis patients. I said by having her instruct dialysis patients, it could destroy his entire study. I told him that Caley had put a plan together for me, and I asked him if he would like a copy of it. He said he told me he would. He said he did not know there was an issue and would discuss this with Dr. Lau. A paper has recently been published titled; *Potential Nutritional Conflicts in Bariatric and Renal Transplant Patients.* Both Dr. Melcher and Dr. Lau were part of the team that authored this paper.

I went by Dr. Melcher's office prior to my meeting with Michael and the nutritionist and signed the necessary papers agreeing to be part of the study for dialysis patients that have bariatric surgery.

I spoke with Michael before the meeting and asked him how many people were in the study. After a bit of probing I found out what I had already had suspected, I was the first in the study. I told Michael, "Someone has to be first, so it might as well be me." The sleeve gastrectomy was scheduled in just five days.

A new chapter in my life was about to begin.

CHAPTER 9

The surgery went off without a hitch. Now the issues with the food were about to begin. I was told for the first two weeks all I would be allowed was liquids. When I returned to my room the first thing they did was bring in a tray of "food". There was sugar-free lemon Jell-O, chicken broth, a protein powder to mix with water, tea and lemonade. Needless to say, I wanted none of this. Tim told me to at least try the protein. I mixed it up, took one sip and that was all I could handle. I did not like the taste of any type of protein drinks.

I have a lot of trouble sleeping in hospitals. At 2:00 AM, I asked the nurse if I could get up and go for a walk. He said that he would go and get a walker for me. We walked around the hallways for about 30 minutes and then he took me back to my room and told me to try and get some sleep. I slept off and on until morning.

The next day they brought in the same "food" items except this time it was beef broth instead of chicken broth and lunch was the same. Right after they brought the lunch tray, the transporter came to take me to dialysis. It was three hours just like my normal days. I told myself I just had to get through the dialysis and then I could go home.

When I returned from dialysis, Tim told me the nurse had said I was not going home until the next day. This did not make me happy. Dr. Lau came by and told me he was keeping me in the hospital because he wanted to make sure there were no problems after having the dialysis treatment. Yet another sleepless night in the hospital. I was released the following day around noon. I asked Dr. Lau if I could swim on April 17th since a new class was starting at Canyon. He said if the stitches were healed and Tim said I could, then it would be all right. He was giving way too much power to Tim!

I went to dialysis on that Friday and everyone was really nervous about how things would go. I told them everything went well with dialysis in the hospital and I had no reason to think it would be any different there. I was more tired than usual, but other than that all went well.

I still was not eating. If I remember correctly I could have light yogurt as long as there were no seeds in it. There was no way I could follow the diet plan that Caley had developed. There was no way I was having any protein drinks. Tim was getting upset with me because I wasn't eating. I told him I would call Michael and see if he had any suggestions.

Michael was not happy with me either. He said, "You have to eat or you will get sick." I told him I could not stand the protein supplement, but he told me to drink it anyway. I listened to Michael about as well as I listened to Tim.

Two days later, I knew I was starving myself, so I took a chance and emailed Dr. Lau. I knew that he was at a conference in Washington, D.C.; however, he told me if I needed him, to email him. I figured there was a slim chance that I would get a response, but I took a chance. In my email I told him that I could not handle the protein supplements and asked if there was anything I could eat, and if not now, then when. To my amazement, I received a response back within 15 minutes. I will never forget what it said; string cheese, tuna – now. Tim went and bought the string cheese and the tuna. The string cheese was fine and I felt better having something in my stomach, small as it was. For dinner I tried having tuna and the minute it hit my stomach it came back up. So much for the tuna. I justified in my mind that if I could have tuna then I should be able to have chicken. Tim and I went to Macaroni Grill. They had a soup that was chicken broth with small pieces of chicken and tiny bits of pasta. That worked.

Michael called to check on me. I told him about the email from Dr. Lau and what it said. For some reason I never mentioned the chicken to him. He was happy that I was at least eating something.

My recovery went smoothly and without any complications. I believe all of the swimming I had been doing had contributed to my speedy recovery.

With a little help from me, all of my stitches were out the morning of April 17. With a little pleading, Tim agreed that it was okay for me to return to swimming. I sent Joe a text message and let him know I would be there that night. It seemed like forever since I had been in the water. Joe took it really easy on me for the first few sessions and then we were back to normal. I was swimming at Lakeridge on days that we did not have class. Once the summer session began it was back to four days a week. My time was filled with swimming and dialysis.

The weight was coming off at a steady pace and by the end of the first month I had lost 18 pounds. Dr. Melcher called and said it was time for my donors to start going through the process to see if they were a match. He told me it would take a while so he wanted to get them to start testing immediately.

I called my sister-in-law, Gail, first and asked her if she was still willing to donate one of her kidneys to me, and she said, "of course." I gave her Stanford's phone number, and she said she would give them a call in the morning. I also called my friend, Carol Carter, and asked her the same thing and she too was still willing to be tested.

My transplant coordinator, Jane Paris, was wonderful. If I called her with questions and she wasn't at her desk, she would call me back the same day. She told me that both Gail and Carol would have different coordinators than me or each other. She said that before the transplant it was all about the donor and after the transplant it would be all about me. She told me she would be there for me whenever I needed her, and she was.

Both Gail and Carol contacted Stanford and got the process going. The process had several steps; therefore it was going to take several months. They were able to do most of the testing near their homes. Gail's would be done in Indiana and Carol's in Nevada. After the first month, Carol was told that since Gail's progress was further along that they were going to suspend her testing pending the results of Gail's.

Gail called to let me know that she had passed the first hurdles. She told me she was going to take it one hurdle at a time.

Dr. Melcher said there would need to be at least a six-month period between surgeries. So, I knew that it would be at least October before the transplant would be considered. Now all I had to do was continue to lose weight and wait for the time to pass. I continued my routine, dialysis three days a week and swimming six to seven days a week.

CHAPTER 10

The mood at dialysis was getting grim as several of the patients had passed away over the last few months. It was always hard on those left behind because it always made people question their own mortality.

I had issues with the dialysis clinic; the machines were breaking down and at times were inaccurate. When machines had problems it meant patients would not get their full treatments. There were other patients scheduled behind them. If the data the machines were producing was inaccurate, for instance if it indicates that three kilos of fluid was removed and then the person would get on the scale and only 1.5 kilos was actually removed, this meant the patient did not have enough fluid removed and could cause additional health issues for them.

Often times there were not adequate staff to handle the patients. The start time was delayed, this even happened with the first shift. Through no fault of their own, dialysis times were cut short because of the next shift coming in. When there was not enough staff, it could compromise the safety of the patients.

After several months of trying to work with the Facilities Administrator and her manager, and getting nowhere, I filed a complaint with the State of California. The State notified the clinic that a complaint had been filed and they would be sending someone to investigate. Although they did not reveal who filed the complaint, I am sure they knew it was me.

All of a sudden things started to improve. The machines were checked for problems, both mechanically and for the data that was retrieved from them, and there now was an abundance of staff.

The State came to investigate about two months after the complaint was made. They spoke with several of the patients. Once their investigation was complete and their report filed, the number of staff was again reduced.

With other patients now complaining and going even further up the chain of command than I did, both the FA and her manager were given other positions within the organization. It is my understanding that the new people in charge were doing a better job, with the patient's welfare in mind. There is now adequate staff to handle the patient's needs.

CHAPTER 11

In July of 2010 I was talking with Katie Hoekstra, a lady I had met at Lakeridge, I told her that I wanted do some volunteer work, but was not sure what I wanted to do. She told me she was part of group of parents that had founded West County Community High School, a small charter high school in Richmond, CA. She said to me they were looking for a couple of people to be on their Board of Directors. She invited me to a meeting and I decided that this was something I would like to do. They asked if I would be their Fundraising Chair. I knew it was going to be a lot of work, but I also thought it was going to be a lot of fun. I did not realize how much money I would need to raise just to meet their operating budget, but I am not one to shy away from a challenge. I had advised them that I was going to be having kidney transplant surgery and that I may need to be away a couple of months. They said they would work with me.

When I first started with them in August of 2010, two seniors, Julia and Daisy, told me they wanted their class to go to Grad Nite at Disneyland. They asked if I could help them raise the money and arrange the trip. I told them that I would be glad to help them. When I spoke with the powers to be at the school, they said there was no way they were going to raise the kind of money they would need to take this trip. They said the kids should plan on going to Santa Cruz or maybe Discovery Kingdom. Both of these venues were within a short driving distance of the school. I talked with the girls and told them how much money they would need to raise and that it was a large sum considering the size of the school, but I would see what I could do to help them make their dream a reality.

When I spoke to the Board of Directors, I told them about the seniors desire to go to Disneyland. I was told that any money they wanted to raise for this trip had to be done outside the school, because the school needed funds to be raised just to operate it. The battle had just begun.

I set up a meeting with the students and their parents to discuss details and the cost of the trip. The cost of the trip was going to be $425.00 per person. This would include the bus ride, the hotel and the tickets into Disneyland, California Theme Park and Universal Studios in Hollywood. I set up a payment plan that would make it affordable for those who wanted to go. Each person had to come up with a down payment the first month and continue to make equal monthly payments until April. Grad Nite would be on May 12, 2011. Most of the students that wanted to go raised funds by selling candy, having car washes and bake sales. They would end up raising enough money that each student would get an envelope with spending money.

Raising money for the school was a lot of work. First I set up pledges from parents who would donate money each month to help the school. In September we had our first big fund raiser of the year. It was a Fiesta Dinner with a raffle and Silent Auction. It was a big success! I would continue to occupy my time with the school, dialysis and swimming as I awaited the hopes of my kidney transplant to become a reality.

In November we were planning what was to be our largest single event for the year, a talent show and pasta dinner. The students, two parents and a teacher provided the night's entertainment. Another group of students, made the different types of pasta. It took the school's leadership class, their teacher and many parents and teachers to make this fundraiser a success. It was night of fun, good food and great entertainment.

CHAPTER 12

Gail kept me updated on her progress and then in August she said she had just received the call saying we were a match. She told me there were still tests that she had to have done at Stanford, but so far so good. They informed her it would take about a month to get the final tests scheduled.

I called and made an appointment with Dr. Melcher to see what would happen next and how much more weight I had to lose. The appointment was set for the end of August. I could hardly wait.

When I went to my appointment I was surprised when Dr. Irene Kim came in and the first thing she said to me was, "Congratulations your BMI is below 40 and you are now eligible for the surgery." I was so happy. I thought I still had 15 more pounds to lose. She told me that she was the fellow, and was now working with Dr. Melcher. I asked her where Dr. Gallo was, and she told me Dr. Gallo was now a fellow in the Liver Transplant Program. I was a bit disappointed at first; however, Dr. Kim turned out to be wonderful.

Dr. Melcher and I discussed the next steps. He told me I had to have some pre-op tests and if everything went well with Gail's tests we should be able to have the surgery in about two months. The timing would be perfect because he wanted at least six months between surgeries.

He said that he had talked with a plastic surgeon, and was 90% sure he was going to take a layer of extra skin off. He felt that this would lessen the risk of infection. I told him whatever he thought was best, was fine with me. He asked me if I realized how much of a risk this surgery was, I told him that I did. He told me to keep swimming and to try to get more weight off if I could.

Gail waited for Stanford to get back to her with the dates for tests. In the beginning of October when she had not heard anything from them, she called her coordinator and asked when they were going to schedule the tests as she needed to make travel plans. She was told that they had to wait for me to get to the required weight before they could schedule any tests. Gail told her that I had become eligible in August. Her coordinator told her they would check it out and get back to her.

Gail and her husband, Dan, were planning on taking a cruise at the end of January, but were putting off booking it because she did not know when the surgery would be. When she still had not heard from Stanford by the third week of October, she figured they were in no hurry, so they booked their cruise.

The thought of having to wait until February to have the transplant, was very upsetting to me. I had been having additional problems with my blood pressure going so low; I nearly passed out a couple of times at dialysis. However, I could not blame Gail and Dan; they couldn't put their life on hold because Stanford couldn't get their act together.

I sent Dr. Melcher an email and asked him if there was any way he could help get the rest of Gail's tests set up. I told him that she had planned a trip for the end of January. I also told him in this email to please tell me I didn't have to wait until February to have the transplant.

The following Sunday, I was at my nephew Danny's home for his birthday BBQ. My cell phone rang. When I picked it up the voice on the other end said, "Linda, this is Dr. Melcher." You could have knocked me over with a feather. He explained to me that he was sorry that the tests had not been set up. He also said that we would have to wait until February. He said that it would be too much of a risk for Gail to travel that close to the transplant. He was very empathetic. I told him I understood. Just the fact that he called touched me deeply.

I called Gail to tell her what Dr. Melcher had said and she told me she was checking on cancelling her trip. I asked her if she was sure she wanted to do this. She said that she would talk with Dan and their travel companions and let me know.

Gail called me the next day and told me that she and Dan had talked and they had made the decision to cancel their trip. She told me that the person she was working with at Stanford called and told her they either wanted her to come out the week of Thanksgiving or on December 6th. She told them it would not be possible for Thanksgiving week since trying to travel that week would be a nightmare. She asked about the week before and was told it was out because the doctors she needed to see were in a conference. They told her they would try and set up the appointments for the week of December 6th. I was so thankful to her and Dan for cancelling their trip.

Gail called me the following day and asked if I was sitting down, I told her I was. She said that the final tests were set up for December 6th, 7th and 8th, and if all went well the transplant surgery would take place on December 10th. It was a good thing I was sitting down because I probably would have stumbled. The emotion that came over me was amazing. To think this was really going to happen and it was all made possible because Gail was willing to donate one of her kidneys to me. I thanked her again for her generosity.

I called Carol to let her know when the transplant was going to happen and thanked her again for offering me one of her kidneys.

I knew that I would have to stay near Stanford for a month after surgery. They wanted me to be close to the hospital in case there were any complications. I called my social worker, Selly, to assist me with housing. She said the apartments near the hospital were one bedroom with a kitchen, bath and small dining room and living room combination. She said they charged $25.00 per day. I told her the price was fine. I asked her if Tim and I could see the apartment, but the she told me that they clean and seal the rooms, so that was not possible. Selly got everything set up for us. She was so wonderful.

I received a call from Stanford letting me know that Dr. Scandling was requiring that I have a stress test on my heart prior to the surgery and they also set me up with my pre-op with Dr. Melcher.

I called my cardiologist, Dr. Anton's office and had them set up the stress test and also a follow up appointment with Dr. Anton to go over the results. After reviewing the results of the test, he told me he would have his assistant fax over the results to Dr. Scandling.

Gail called and said that she and Dan would be driving out the day after Thanksgiving and would be stopping at family and friend's homes along the way. Their anticipated date to arrive would be Saturday, December 4th. She gave me her test schedule and I told her I was meeting with Dr. Melcher on December 7th. Gail and Dan arrived as scheduled and her final tests began on Monday.

I met with Dr. Melcher, and he went over how things would happen. They would take Gail in early in the morning and remove one of her kidneys. While they were in surgery with her, they would then begin to prep me. After they completed her surgery, the transplant team would take a rest. He would come in and see me just prior to surgery and then they would begin. He again reminded me that this was a risky surgery, explaining possibility of infections that could happen around the wound area and also a possibility that there could be a viral or bacterial infection. I told him I would be just fine and there would be no infections. He said that I did not know that. I told him that I did.

Since my end stage renal diagnosis, my way of handling things was to try to always be positive. I knew I was in Dr. Melcher's very capable hands. I also knew in my heart there would be no infections.

Prior to surgery I met with two of the transplant coordinators. They gave me a transplant recipient teaching manual that we went over chapter by chapter. It contained information about the anti-rejection medicine I would need to take for the rest of my life, how to avoid complications and the visits that were required to the clinic after surgery.

There was a chapter on self-care, advising me to:

- Drink 64 to 96 ounces of fluid a day.
- Weigh myself at the same time each morning
- Take my temperature twice daily
- Record my blood pressure twice daily
- Record blood sugar levels four times a day
- Follow my medication instructions
- Note any changes and report to the Transplant Team

Plus all of the information you would possibly need to know about post-transplant care.

They also told me that Jane would no longer be my transplant coordinator, since she only handles patients prior to the transplant. I was a little sad when I heard this, because Jane had been wonderful with me the entire time we worked together.

Gail received the official word on Wednesday that she was cleared for surgery and that we needed to be at the hospital on Thursday at 1:00 in the afternoon to check in. She was told to make sure we had a nice lunch because we would not be eating anything until after surgery. We went to a wonderful Italian restaurant in San Carlos.

Since I was to stay near Stanford for a month and Tim would have to return to work the week after Christmas, it was set up so Dar would stay one week with me, my friend Sue Cox would take the second and Joy and Aunt Patty would split the last week. They would be there through the week and Tim would come on the weekend.

My Most Amazing Journey Was About To Begin

CHAPTER 13

Gail and I checked into the hospital promptly at 1:00 PM on Thursday, December 9, 2010. After completing all of the admission papers, we were assigned private rooms next to each other.

Selly came by around 2:30 and she and Tim went over to secure the apartment. When Tim came back he said he had already unpacked but he would have to go to the grocery store before I got out of the hospital.

Gail had been asked to take part in a study for older people who were donating kidneys. She called it her "old people's study". They gave her fluids through an IV as well as drinking water and they were taking blood and measuring her urine on a regular basis. They were going to look at her kidney function prior to her donating a kidney and they would repeat the test in six months to a year to see what changes had occurred.

Dr. Melcher came in and said that Gail's kidneys were on the small side so my creatinine levels would be slightly elevated. He once again reminded me of the risks, his biggest concerns were infections that may occur, post-transplant. I told him not to worry there would be no infections. He appeared to be a little irritated with me and told me he did not think I was taking this serious enough and did not understand the risks. I told him, "Oh I understand the risks."

When Dr. Melcher left, Tim repeated the same concerns as Dr. Melcher. I told Tim, "Look I can have the transplant and everything will be alright, I can die on the table or I can die a little each day I have dialysis. Which is worse?"

There was no more talk about me not understanding the risks.

The conversation with Dr. Melcher and Tim upset me a bit. Being positive is how I had dealt with this illness each step of the way. This was not a time to become pessimistic, especially now with so much at stake.

Dr. Melcher came in a little later and said the surgery would go a little longer because Gail's kidneys had an extra artery that had to be attached. This was no problem for me because I was going to be asleep. He also told me that he had decided to take the extra skin in the area where they were going to transplant the kidney. He said it wasn't going to be pretty, but should reduce the chances for infection. I told him "Oh well there goes my ever wearing a bikini!" We all laughed and he said he would see me the next day prior to surgery.

Tim left the hospital around 9:00 PM and said he would be back the next morning before they took Gail to surgery.

I talked with Gail about the conversation with both Dr. Melcher and Tim and how it upset me. After we talked for a while, we came to the conclusion that they were both very concerned about the risk. When I went back to my room I was feeling much better.

The following morning at 6:00 AM, they came and took Gail to prep her for surgery. My niece, Seana, and her friend, Gina, were at the hospital around 9:00 AM. They wanted to spend some time with me prior to surgery. I was so glad they had come. This also gave Tim the opportunity to spend some time with Dan, as Gail's surgery had already begun.

This was a difficult day for Tim. Not only was I in surgery, his sister was as well, and there was always that chance that something could go wrong with one or both of us.

Seana, Gina and I played a game on the television. It was a different version of Yatzee, but it helped the time pass as we waited for them to come and take me to the pre-op. Tim came back a little later and joined us in the game.

They came at 1:00 PM to take me to pre-op. They told Tim, Seana and Gina that they could come with me but had to stay in the waiting room until they had me settled in and they would come get them; however only one person at a time could be in the pre-op room.

Once in the pre-op room, they took all of my vitals and asked a lot of questions. When they finished all of their preliminary work, they let Seana and Gina come in for a few minutes one at a time. Then Tim came in and he was there with me until they took me to surgery. The anesthesiologist came and introduced himself and told me the nurse was going to give me something to relax me and when I was in the operating room they would insert the IV's. He told me not to worry they would take good care of me. I told him I was not worried at all.

Dr. Melcher came in and said there was a beautiful kidney waiting for me in the operating room. He told Tim and me, that Gail was in the recovery room next door and all went well with her surgery. He was going to go and take a break before they began my surgery.

I do not remember being wheeled into the operating room. The last thing I remember was Dr. Kim being upset because the operating room was not ready and she was going to find out why!

After the surgery, I woke up in the recovery room and was told that my family could see me once I was back in my room. Dr. Melcher came in and told me the surgery went a little longer than expected but that everything went just fine and he would see me in the morning. He said he had already talked with Tim. The surgery was over at around ten at night and I was back in my room around eleven. The nurse told everyone they could come in after she got me settled.

Seana and Gina came in to say goodnight and said they were going home. Seana said she would be back with Larry and their son, William, the day after Christmas.

When Tim came in he told me that the extra skin that Dr. Melcher removed during surgery weighed five pounds. He said that Dr. Melcher said not let anyone take out my staples. Tim looked exhausted, I told him to go back to the apartment and get some sleep. He told me he would be back in the morning.

The nurse came in and out through the evening checking my vitals and making sure I was okay. She gave me pain medicine when I needed it, which fortunately was not often. Like most nights, anytime I am in the hospital I do not get much sleep.

They brought in breakfast and of course I wanted no part of it, but I had no choice. I had to eat in order to take my pills. I had to take 17 different medications; of those, three were anti-rejection.

Tim came back early in the morning. He said that he had decorated the apartment for Christmas. We had brought a small tree and a few of our favorite decorations. That was so kind of him; he knew how hard it was going to be for me to be away from the family on Christmas.

Dr. Melcher came in the following morning with an entourage of students and indicated they would be putting me on a gradual dosage of prednisone and that I would end up taking a small dosage the rest of my life. He also told that me I would be on a sliding scale of insulin which I would also probably be on for the rest of my life.

Gail and I were on opposite sides of the hospital. I called her to see how she was doing. She was having problems with nausea. She was not use to taking pain medication and she was experiencing a little discomfort at the incision area. Other than that she felt fine. She told me she would have Dan wheel her down later to visit. It was too far for her to try and walk.

My days following the surgery were routine. I had to learn the names and the doses of the medication I was now taking. I was provided a long list that told me what to take and when to take them.

The hard part was learning to drink fluids again. After three and a half years of taking in no more than 32 ounces a day, I was now required to drink 64 to 96 ounces a day to keep myself hydrated.

On the Monday following surgery, Tim found out that the company he had been working for had decided to close the entire operation in the office where he worked. The fortunate things were that they first put everyone on paid administrative leave for two months and then his severance package would take him through mid-May and the health benefits would go until the end of May. However all of the employees had to work until the end of the year. It was a blow to both of us; at least we were covered for medical through May.

Gail was discharged from the hospital on the Monday following the surgery. She and Dan were going to stay in the Stanford area until her appointment on Thursday and then they would be staying at our home until Christmas Day.

Dr. Kim and Dr. Busque came in and told me that I would be able to leave the hospital the next day, after they gave me my last medication that took six hours through the IV. That would be number four of four. I really hated it because it made me feel like I was ready to start climbing the walls. Dr. Melcher recently told me that was because of the steroids they gave me prior to giving me the medication. Dr. Busque told me that they were going to reduce the prednisone to five milligrams effective that day.

The next day when the doctors came in they told me that the nurse coordinators would be in to go over all of the medications that had been delivered from the pharmacy. They said they would see me on Thursday in the clinic.

The most difficult part of the surgery was having the IV's in my neck. There was so much tape and it was very irritating. I am sure the steroids had something to do with that irritation.

Eating was still a problem for me. Nothing tasted good and I was not hungry. I had no choice but to eat in the morning, because of the medication. Other than that most of the trays went back.

The next afternoon, after they finished the final round of the IV medication, Becky, the nurse coordinators came in and to go over the medications I would be taking.

She reminded me that I had to:

- Weigh myself every morning
- Take my blood pressure three times a day
- Check my blood sugar four times a day
- Check my temperature twice a day

Everything had to be recorded on two different charts and was to be reviewed with the transplant staff at each clinic appointment. They indicated there was a number to call 24 hours a day if I had any problems. Everything I needed was on the medication list.

The nurse finally came in and took the IV out of my neck and told me I would have to lie still for 30 minutes. Then I could be discharged.

The nurse called for a wheel chair and said they were backed up in the transport department. So now all I had to do was wait. While I sat there waiting, Dr. Lau dropped by to see how I was doing. He had told me previously that he would come by to see me when I had the transplant surgery. It was nice to see him.

Finally after what seemed to be hours, they took me downstairs where Tim was waiting.

CHAPTER 14

The apartment was a very short drive from the hospital. We were on the third floor. When I walked into the apartment I was somewhat disappointed. For some reason pictures on the internet never look like the real thing. However, Tim had it decorated really nice. There was a rocker/recliner, a television with a 16" screen, a sofa and a dining room table and in the bedroom there were two twin beds. There was also a smell that turned my stomach. It must have been the type of cleaning products they used.

Tim called his brother, Tom and let him know that I had the transplant surgery. Tom said he and Joyce would be there to visit on Friday.

I was very uncomfortable at the apartment and the thought of having to stay there for 30 days was inconceivable.

Tim would get upset because I ate very little. I would tell him I was doing my best. He would help me shower each morning and each afternoon. He would clean the area where the stiches were. He changed the bandages a couple of times a day. As usual, he took very good care of me.

On Thursday, Gail and I both had appointments in the clinic. I was surprised to see that Dr. Busque was there instead of Dr. Melcher. Dr. Kim was there, she was so wonderful! Dr. Busque told me that everything looked good and if there were any changes in the medication, they would call me during the afternoon. He told me to make an appointment for Monday. For a while I would be coming to the clinic twice a week for labs and to see one of the doctors.

My nephew, Danny, came for a visit on Thursday. He stayed for a few hours, which gave Tim some time to do some shopping. It was so good to see him, as it always is.

Tom and Joyce came around noon on Friday. I called Gail and she told me that she and Dan would be over in about an hour. When Gail and Dan arrived, we decided we would have sandwiches for lunch. Tim, Dan, Tom and Joyce went to the deli and Gail and I stayed at the apartment. I told Gail that I was going to ask the doctor on Monday if I could go home. She said he would never let me do that. I told her, it never hurts to ask.

On Sunday, Tim and I were watching a movie and I told him that tomorrow when I saw the doctor, I was going to ask him if I could go home. He said the same thing as Gail. I told him I was going to ask anyway.

I was not happy staying at the apartment. For me it was uncomfortable and it smelled bad. I missed my three dogs and I really wanted to be home for Christmas. This was my great-niece Ella's first Christmas. Everyone was going to be at Joy's on Christmas Eve. The kids were going to be so much fun, William, and the triplets, Samantha, Kaiya and Daphne.

The next morning when we were on our way to the clinic for my labs and doctor's appointments, I kept saying in my mind, let it be Dr. Busque today. I felt I had a better chance of getting a "yes" answer from him.

We were taken into the examining room and I asked the nurse who was going to be the doctor that day and she said Dr. Busque. I told Tim, "Don't you say anything when I ask him!" Tim gave me one of his looks and then told me the doctor was going to say no.

When the Dr. Busque was examining me, he asked me how I was feeling and I told him "Good, can I go home?" He asked me how far away home was and I told him. He asked me if I would be able to keep my appointments twice a week and I told him I would. He said, "Okay you can go home." I thanked him. As I was waiting for the nurse to bring in some supplies for me to take home, my phone rang. It was Gail.

She asked if I had seen the doctor yet and I told her I had and that I was coming home. Tim was not too happy about this at first.

We went back to the apartment so Tim could start packing things up. As I was helping him take the decorations off the tree, he asked me if I expected him to put this back up when we got home. I told him no. I was just happy to be going home.

When we arrived home in the late afternoon, two of my dogs, JuJu and Kasie were so happy to see me, it took my youngest dog, Grady a minute and then he went a little crazy. I was so happy to see them.

It was so good to be home!

CHAPTER 15

Gail and I both had appointments on the Thursday before Christmas. The doctors told her she would have to stay in California for two weeks following the surgery. She was also told she would have to give herself a shot every day that she was on the road to prevent blood clots. Since she was not one to give herself a shot, she elected Dan to do this job. She was given the clearance to leave. I made my appointment for Monday.

One of the side effects from one of the anti-rejection medications I was taking was that I was always cold. The heater would be on 72 and I would have two blankets on me.

During the afternoon, on Christmas Eve, Gail and Dan asked Tim and I to join them and their daughter, Gayleen, and her two children, Alex and Josh for lunch at Skates By the Bay, a very nice restaurant in the Berkeley Marina. The food was good. We had a great view and such great company.

After we left Skates, Tim and I went to Joy's to spend the rest of the afternoon and part of the evening with my side of the family. It was so much fun watching five little ones open up their presents with the help of their parents.

Much to my surprise, I made it through the day with little pain. I was tired, but it was a good tired, if there was such a thing.

Gail and Dan left the next morning. They were going to spend time with Dan's children and their families before heading to Indiana.

I was sure going to miss them! I will be forever grateful for the gift she has given me.

Tim and I spent a quiet day at home for Christmas. We opened our presents and watched a couple of movies. I was very thankful that Dr. Busque had let me come home.

The next week, Tim's company said everyone had to come in and help box things up. Joy took me to Stanford on Monday and all went well with my visit. I was surprised that I had not seen Dr. Melcher in the clinic. I asked where he was and was told that he was taking some much needed time off because he had covered for Dr. Busque, who had been on a sabbatical for six weeks.

It seemed like my medication was adjusted each time I went to the clinic. I was told this was normal. Dr. Busque took me off insulin because I needed so little and sometimes I didn't need it at all. He put me on a low dosage pill. He told me to make my next appointment for Thursday.

After I received my lab results, I would call Gail to keep her updated on how I was doing.

On Thursday it was my Aunt Patty's turn to take me to Stanford. Dr. Kim and Dr. Busque both said the wound looked good and was healing. There were no signs of infection. I asked Dr. Kim if she thought it would be alright if I got my nails done. She told me that she did not see a problem doing that, in fact she thought it would do me good.

I made my appointment for Monday for the clinic, then I called my manicurist and asked her if she had an opening and if anyone else there had time to do Aunt Patty's nails. She set up our appointments for 3:00. At 2:30, I check my messages because I thought I would have heard from someone at Stanford by now. I noticed I had two messages, and just as I was about to check them, I received a call from Becky at Stanford. She said that I needed to return to Stanford and be admitted in to the hospital as soon as possible. She said the doctors wanted me under a 23-hour observation. When I asked what was going on she said they did not like my labs and I would learn more when I got to the hospital. She said to come through the regular hospital admitting, that they were expecting me.

I called Tim and let him know I was on my way to the hospital, not sure why, but that I was staying overnight. He said to wait for him. Tim, Aunt Patty and I left for the hospital in the midst of rush hour traffic.

I was admitted to the hospital for observation around 6:00 PM and was in my new accommodations for the night shortly thereafter.

The nurse came in and said they were going to have the trauma nurse come in and attempt to put an IV in me. They needed to start me on fluids as well as an antibiotic. She said I was dehydrated, had a urinary tract infection and would need two units of blood. The first thing I told her was that I wanted to see a doctor because I had questions about the blood transfusion. The resident on staff came in and explained about the transfusion and the reason I needed one right away. It appeared I was losing blood at a rather rapid pace. He said Dr. Busque told him the transfusion would fix the problem. He said the kidney needed more blood in order to produce more on its own.

The trauma nurse came in and attempted to get a regular IV in my left arm. They could not use my right arm because the fistula was there. After trying several places and finally blowing one of my veins, she was able to get a juvenile IV in my arms. This would enable them to get the fluids and the antibiotic going, but was not sufficient for the blood transfusion.

They called one of the paramedics from the helicopter trauma unit and after he blew a vein he said he was not going to hurt me anymore. He said it looked to him that one of the doctors was going to have to put an IV in my neck. I was not looking forward to that. This was the first time during the entire transplant experience that I was nervous about something.

The nurse told me the doctors would not be in until the morning and that she was not going to be able to do the blood transfusion until then.

Tim and Aunty Patty decided to spend the night. They brought in a rollaway bed and put it next to my bed. Aunt Patty slept there and Tim made a makeshift bed in the lobby.

The next day Dr. Busque and Dr. Kim came in to see me. Dr. Busque explained everything that was going on and why I needed the transfusion. Dr. Kim told me she would be putting the IV in my neck. I asked Dr. Busque if I could go home after the transfusion was completed. It was New Year's Eve and I did not want to start the New Year off in the hospital. He said no problem.

When Dr. Kim was ready to insert the IV, she asked Tim and my aunt to leave the room. They were happy to oblige. She told me to lie very still and everything would be just fine. When she was finished putting the needles in I realized that I had nothing to be worried about. She had been so wonderful through this entire process. I will never forget her.

We got home around 7:00 PM New Year's Eve. Aunt Patty decided to go on home. Tim and I spent a quiet evening at home. We both woke up just in time for the year to turn from 2010 to 2011.

It had been the most amazing year.

CHAPTER 16

I went to the clinic on January 2, 2011 and in walked Dr. Melcher. I asked him if he still worked here. We all laughed. It was really good to see him. I was surprised that Dr. Kim was not with him. He said she had finished her fellowship with him and was now working at the Lucile Packard Children's Hospital. He said that Dr. Gallo was back to finish her fellowship.

Things were going really well, so they changed my visits to the clinic to once a week instead of twice. My anti-rejection medication changed every time I had labs. But so far so good.

My emotions seemed to be all over the place. This was very unusual for me. I once again contacted Jeff and he was able to help me through it. Talking it out with him, helped me realize that I had gone from a very structured and routine schedule, to being able to pretty much do what I wanted to and that was hard to figure out how to handle this new freedom.

I was getting stronger every day and now I came to the Kidney Transplant Clinic every other week.

I went to my former dialysis center to visit my friends I had not seen since before the surgery. It was so good to see everyone. I visited with six of the patients. We talked about how they were doing and they were anxious to hear how I was doing.

First I spoke with Jamie. He was in the chair next to me for several months and we would visit during most treatments. Then came Brenda, she was a very nice lady who sat kitty corner from me. Next was, Mr.

Robertson (Bill). He had always been one of my favorite people there. He is such a special person. He had tears in his eyes when he saw me. We talked for a while and he told me he was talking with the VA Hospital and was hoping that soon something would happen for him. I wished him the very best and I moved on to Edward. We would exchange good mornings as he passed my chair, and he would comment on which book I was reading. He told me that he was working with Davis and thought he might be able to get a transplant soon. I wished him well and told him that if for some reason things did not work out there to contact Stanford. I told him how pleased I was with them. Then there was GaGa. She has been on dialysis for 20 years and even had a baby during this time.

I spoke with all of the nurses and techs that were there. They all told me how good I was looking and how happy they were to see me and to make sure I came back again to visit.

Leah, my nurse while I was at the dialysis center was walking me towards the door and told me that if we didn't wake the other Brenda up she would be really mad at her. She told me that Brenda kept asking about me. Brenda sat in the chair on the other side of me. When I spoke with her, she told me she was being sent to a hospital in Southern California for "Desensitization". What this means is:

> By nature, your body doesn't react well when foreign objects are introduced into it. It's safe to say that your body would consider a new kidney to be foreign. Your immune system would produce organ-rejecting antibodies that would guarantee transplant failure without a desensitization treatment protocol prior to surgery.
>
> Of the 90,000 or so people on the national transplant waiting list, it's estimated that as many as 30% of them are hypersensitive to the markers on the surface of donor kidneys, therefore requiring the desensitization treatment protocol prior to surgery.

Brenda said that she would need to make five or six trips to Southern California, just for desensitization. (I was surprised that they would send her that far away from home, especially now that I found out that

Stanford could perform the same protocol.) She said if everything went well she could get her transplant towards the end of the year. I wished her well and told her I would be back again to visit. It was nice to see everyone again.

Stanford is one of the few medical facilities in the United States with an active desensitization program.

CHAPTER 17

In February I heard that Stanford had a new President. I decided it was time to write a letter to let him know how great the Kidney Transplant Team was. Below is a copy of the letter I hand delivered to Stanford, I also copied Dr. Scandling, since he was the head of the unit.

Mr. Amir Dan Rubin
Stanford Hospital and Clinics
300 Pasteur Drive
Palo Alto, CA 94304

February 15, 2011

Dear Mr. Rubin:

Please let me take a moment of your time to recognize the great Kidney Transplant team you have there at Stanford, as they are second to none.

I have in the past dealt with both UCSF and Davis Kidney transplant teams and there is no comparison in the professionalism, the care or the concern your staff provides.

I started my journey with Stanford in December of 2009 when I called and asked to be evaluated by your transplant team. I met with Dr. John Scandling and his team. He understood my frustration as I had lost 190 pounds prior to our meeting and still had more to lose before the transplant could be performed. I asked him an unusual question and that was would any of the extra skin that I have be considered as part of the weight that I was carrying. He gave me an honest answer, that he had not had that questioned asked of him before. He examined me and I think was a bit surprised that I had so much of it.

He indicated that this was not his call but that of Dr. Marc Melcher who was the kidney transplant surgeon. He said he would talk to him about seeing me but that he usually did not see patients until closer to the actual transplant date. He said he would talk with him about meeting with me.

How fortunate for me that Dr. Melcher agreed to meet with me. On that fateful day in January, I met with both he and his Fellow, Dr. Amy Gallo. He actually asked me about my story. You see I was diagnosed with end stage renal disease along many other problems in July of 2007. At that time, I weighed 446 pounds, could only walk a few feet and would be totally out of breath. When I saw him on that day I weighed 256 pounds and was swimming 50 to 60 laps 5 to 6 days a week.

I told him my story. He examined me and we determined that I did still have more weight to lose. We decided on my having the sleeve gastrectomy and referred me to Dr. James Lau in the bariatric department. Stanford should be proud to have him on staff. He is another wonderful and caring doctor.

We discussed the study that they were performing on dialysis patients that have bariatric surgery and I agreed to be part of the study.

To make a long story shorter, I lost the additional weight that was needed and I had the transplant on December 10, 2010. My sister-in-law, Gail Bridges-Rea was my doner.

The care and concern that we both received before, during and after our stay at the hospital was remarkable.

Dr. Melcher, Dr. Stephan Busque, Dr. Irene Kim (Fellow), Dr. Amy Gallo (Fellow), Selly Castillo (my Social Worker), Jane Paris (my Transplant Coordinator prior to surgery), the nurses I had right after surgery Ryan (day shift) and Valerie (night shift) and the other countless staff that is part of the entire transplant team have my highest praise and will always have my sincerest gratitude.

Thank you for your time.

Sincerely,

Linda Nigma
Kidney Transplant Recipient

Cc: Dr. John Scandling

Unfortunately, people have a tendency to complain when things do not go their way, but somehow forget to praise when things do.

I had an appointment on that day and Dr. Busque was in. He told me that now that I was doing so well, after my next appointment he would refer me to nephrology and then they would send me back to my own nephrologist. I told him I did not want to return to my doctor that I wanted Dr. Scandling to be my doctor. He said that he did not think Dr. Scandling was taking on any new patients because he had a very busy schedule. I asked him if he could refer me to Dr. Scandling. He indicated I could see Dr. Scandling in two weeks and ask him.

In the middle of February, my friend Theresa told me that there was a possibility that there may be a temporary contract position at the company I worked for prior to my disability. She said the position would be perfect for me and I would be perfect for the position. Theresa said that they could work it out so that I could ease back into the workforce. She said it would be 25 to 40 hours a week depending on how I felt. She also said I could work at home most of the time. This would be perfect if it could all be worked out.

When Dr. Scandling walked into the room at my next appointment on March 1st, he first thanked me for writing the letter and then again for bringing in the chocolates. He said the staff enjoyed them. He went over my labs and then started to tell me what would happen next. He said he would be referring me back to my doctor and then he would see me in three months. I told him I did not want to go back to my doctor that I wanted him to be my doctor. He asked where I lived and how far away that was. Then he asked if I had a PCP that I could see. I answered his questions, and he told me that he would be my doctor. He said he would need to see me more often and we set the next appointment for one month. He also told me that I would need to continue my labs every two weeks. I felt much better knowing that Dr. Scandling and Stanford were going to be reviewing my labs.

Dr. Scandling told me that I could return to swimming, but to take it slow. He told me I could exercise, however if I started to feel pain that I needed to stop.

I went to the end of the hall to see if by chance Dr. Melcher was in the clinic and sure enough he was. We visited for a little while and then I left so he could continue seeing patients.

I tried going back to swimming but because the weather was so cold and rainy it was hard to get into that outdoor pool. I was still feeling cold most of the time.

I sent Joe an email letting him know how things were going since the transplant. In his reply he told me he was going to be teaching the spring session at Canyon on Tuesday and Thursday night's beginning in April. I told him I would contact Canyon and set up private lessons for the entire spring session. I thought this was a good way to get back to swimming and the water was always extra warm.

Everything continued as usual with the exception of some anxiety I was feeling. Jeff and I talked about it in length and although we could not pinpoint exactly where this was coming from, we decided that perhaps the best approach to getting past this was to do meditation, to just clear my mind and relax. I had used meditation in the past to deal with some of the issues I had when dealing with grief. This helped lessen the feelings I was having. Sometimes just talking with him was all I needed.

Going back to work proved to be a challenge. With the flexibility of working at home and the reduced number of hours it was manageable. I still got tired but then after resting I was ready to continue working. I was grateful to be working again.

I was asked to work with another group within the unit two days a week. This would require that I be in the office on Tuesday and Thursday. I explained to the manager that I would need the flexibility to be late on days that I had appointments or lab work and to be able to leave early on days that I might get tired. He told me he had no problem with this.

My swimming classes began in early April, 2011. It was so good to see Joe and everyone else that worked at Canyon. The pool was warm and inviting. The most difficult part of returning to swimming was getting the breathing down. Joe took it easy on me the first session and then started pushing me later on which helped get the breathing part back on track. Still for some reason it was hard for me to get back to swimming and exercise. I would go to my classes and maybe to the gym one more day during the week. I knew eventually I would get back in full swing. I just was not prepared to do that at this time.

When I met with Dr. Scandling in April and told him I was working, he had that look of concern on his face. I told him about the flexibility and he seemed a little less concerned. He then told me to be sure and take it easy. He said that he was pleased with how things were going and we decided that I would come back again in mid-June. My labs were to continue to be once a month.

CHAPTER 18

It was almost time to take the 2011 Senior Class to Grad Nite at Disneyland. We had our final meeting the week before the trip. I let the students know I would be able to join them. They were very happy about this. I went over Disney's rules with them and then told them my own set of rules. I let them know what type of behavior I expected from them and they all said they understood and agreed. They were so excited; the students, the teachers and the parents. The trip was just one week away.

When the day finally arrived for the kids to leave for Disneyland, Tim and I met with the bus driver at 5:00 AM. Everyone was on time. There were four chaperones on the bus, two parents Leticia and Billy and two teachers Miss Crystal and Mr. Gary. Tim and I drove our car and told them we would meet them at the hotel.

We were staying at the Anaheim Desert Inn and Suites which was right across the street from the entrance to Disneyland. I had made reservations for suites that held eight in each room which included one chaperone. I had arranged a pizza party for them at 5:00.

Grad Nite would begin at 8:00 PM at the California Adventure Park. This park is adjacent to Disneyland and is roughly half the size. Tim and I walked both parks. The last four times we were at Disney World, I had to rent scooters to get around the parks. It was amazing to be able to walk! At 10:30 PM everyone went to Disneyland and we were there until 5:00 AM. I made it through the entire evening without a problem.

The next morning at 9:00, we took them to Universal Studios. Not much sleep for anyone, but they all had a great time. To be able to not only stay up all night, but to be able to walk all three parks was a great accomplishment.

Tim and I decided to stay an additional night in Anaheim and I called our friend, Kevin Craig, who we had not seen in years. Kevin and his wife, Bobbi, (who I had not yet met) lived near Disneyland. He sang a few songs for us from his band, *1st Rodeo*'s, just-released CD, "*There Goes the Neighborhood*". Then we were off to dinner.

We came back to their home after dinner and Kevin sang a couple more songs for us. He has such a great voice. We had a wonderful visit with them. It was a fun trip for us; I got to see just how far I had come since the transplant and we got to meet up with a very special friend.

I went to the senior's graduation and one of the students, Daniel, thanked me in his speech during the ceremony for making his dream of going to Disneyland come true.

My term as volunteer with the school was coming to an end.

Through all our efforts (parents, students, teachers and myself), we were able to raise more money than the school had ever raised previously. In addition to the Fiesta Dinner and Talent Show, we had Top-Cook Competition between parents and a raffle where the parents and teachers were asked to sell tickets raised the most money of any of the fundraisers that we had.

The final fundraiser I was involved in was on my last day as fundraising chair. It was dollar days ($1.00 each to get in, park, purchase hotdogs, beer, water and sodas) at Golden Gate Fields on Memorial Day. Golden Gate Fields is a local thorough-bred horse racing park. We had previously worked two other days; however this was going to be their largest crowd of the season. I had a feeling since school was already out that we were going to be short on volunteers, so I recruited Tim to help us out. As it turned out there were only six there. Tim and Linda Asher and Billy Asher poured over 2,500 cups of beer and Carmen, Janae and I, served the beer, more than 3,000 hotdogs and countless cases of soda and water over a five-hour period. We never got a break and never sat down. We raised over $1,000 for the school.

It was an enjoyable and a great experience having held the position but now it was time to move on to something new.

CHAPTER 19

There are several groups available to help educate and support dialysis patients. Selly told me about two organizations; Renal Support Network (RSN) and The Western Pacific Renal Network. Here is a just a glimpse at what these two organizations do:

RNS

This is their Mission Statement:

"The Renal Support Network (RSN) is a nonprofit, patient-focused, patient-run organization that provides non-medical services to those affected by chronic kidney disease (CKD). RSN strives to help patients develop their personal coping skills, special talents, and employability by educating and empowering them (and their family members) to take control of the course and management of the disease. A vital role of RSN is to provide lawmakers and policymakers with the patients' perspective on the needs and capabilities of people with CKD."

RSN also has a team of speakers that are part of their PEPP Patient Speakers Program. The speakers work with patient and professional groups to enhance awareness about chronic kidney disease. Anyone who would like a speaker to educate others about kidney disease or would like a speaker for a healthcare meeting, please go online to: rsnhope.org and request a speaker. If anyone would like to contact them, their support line their HOPEline number is: 800-579-1970 or their website is: rsnhope.org.

<u>The Western Pacific Renal Network, LLC</u>

The mission of the Western Pacific Renal Network, LLC is to facilitate improvement of quality of care provided to ESRD patients.

- *Improve the quality and safety of dialysis related services provided for individuals with ESRD*
- *Improve patient's perception of care and experience of care, and resolve patient's grievances.*

You can find more information on this organization at their website: www.esrdnet17.org. This organization is sponsored by Medicare and Medical.

These are just two of several organizations that support both the patients with end stage renal disease and their families. To find addition organizations, go on the internet and look under "dialysis patients support groups". There is even support group for caregivers, their website is: www.thefamilycaregiver.org.

I bring these names to light because the entire time that I was on dialysis I did not know any of these organization existed. Since my transplant, I have talked with some of these organizations and found that they may also have been helpful for me had I know about them.

There are also support groups for people with other chronic illnesses. Check online for their website information.

CHAPTER 20

Exercise was the key to how quickly I recovered from both surgeries but it was not easy to get started again after having the transplant. I was getting stronger every day it was time to start including exercise back in my life. I decided I wanted to change my routine. Instead of going back to swimming six to seven days a week, I began a new routine of going swimming three days and doing weight training three days a week in the gym.

It is said that if you do something consistently for 30 days it will become a habit. That has proven true for me.

I called and spoke with Dolores Lopez, a personal trainer at Lakeridge and asked her if she could work with me. We determined that since I did not need someone to be there with me all the time that twice a month would work to our best advantage. She showed me how to use the equipment and set up a personalized program, which included various types of machines and weight training. I also included walking on the treadmill before and after my program.

I had now been back on this exercise routine for over 30 days and it had become routine again, as well as a very important part of my life.

Swimming isn't for everyone and exercising in a gym is not always possible for an individual. All I can do is stress the importance of doing some type of exercise every day. Exercise starts by taking one step at a time and adding more steps as the days go by. As "they" (whoever they may be) say, walking is the best exercise. If a person has difficulty getting started or believes that they cannot include exercise in their life, they could try walking. Just stepping out their door and walking a few steps is a great way to begin. Maybe walk to the neighbor's house, and do that for a couple days. Then try adding a few more steps and before they know it, they are walking to the end of the block. My friend Dianne said she and her neighbor started out walking just 15 minutes up the street and 15 minutes back. They did this for a week and then realized that they were walking a little further each day.

For some people who have problems with their knees or their back, walking tends to be uncomfortable. Water walking in a swimming pool could be a good solution. Most YMCA's have a pool and the cost is minimal. The water takes the pressure off of the joints, making extended movement nearly pain free. Everyone should be able to find a form of exercise that is not only beneficial but fun. Whether it is sitting in a chair and moving their legs and/or arms or running a marathon, the important thing is to move. It could add years to a person's life.

PRIOR TO STARTING ANY EXERCISE PROGRAM ALWAYS CHECK WITH YOUR DOCTOR FIRST

CHAPTER 21

I realize how fortunate I was to have Gail offer me one of her kidneys. There are no words to ever express the gratitude and love I feel for her. I would like to help people become more aware not only how CKD affects the patient's lives but their families as well. To let people know that in San Francisco Bay Area where I live, once a person is placed on the kidney transplant list to receive a kidney the wait is now over eight years. In many cases by the time a person's name reaches the top of the list to receive a kidney they are too ill to be able withstand the surgery to receive the kidney that has become available for them.

Donors are in desperate need. I urge people that may know someone in need of a kidney to consider becoming a donor. Please keep in mind most dialysis patients would never dare ask a person for something so precious. I know I would have never asked anyone.

The following information was taken from the Stanford Hospital and Clinics _Kidney Transplant Program – Guide To Understanding Transplant._ This is a brochure that is available by contacting the Kidney Transplant Program.

Stanford protects the privacy of every potential donor. Both the recipient and the donor will be assigned separate transplant coordinators and social workers. Medical information will not be shared.

Medical costs of the evaluation and donation are the responsibility of the recipient's medical insurance company.

There are options for incompatible donors. Even though you as a family member or a friend may not be a match, there are additional programs available.

> ***Paired Exchange:*** With paired-organ donations you as the donor can exchange your kidney with the living donor/recipient pair to create two compatible pairs. While that it is true that your kidney with not go directly to your family member or friend, your exchange will allow for two compatible transplants
> ***Chain Transplants:*** Donor chains work similarly to paired donations in that they take advantage healthy but willing donors that are otherwise incompatible. A non-directed donor is someone who offers to donate a kidney without a designated recipient, but with the explicit wish to donate to someone in need of a transplant.

For more information on Paired Exchange and Chain Transplants, please see Dr. Melcher's publication at:

> *knol.google.com/k/paired-exchange-kidney-donation-donor-chains-in-kidney-transplantation*

Again I stress there just are not enough kidneys to meet the increasing demand. According to the United Network For Organ Sharing, as of late 2010, there were 93,000 waiting list candidates. This is up from the 84,000 that were registered as of April 2010. The numbers appear to increase daily. Again, the wait for a kidney transplant in the San Francisco Bay Area is 8.5 years!

You can make a difference in family members; a friend's or evens a stranger's life.

Potential donors can begin the evaluation process by contacting Stanford's living donor coordinator at 650-736-0795.

One of my goals is to help bring awareness of the need for Living Donors to the public; with the hope this will make a difference in someone's life.

<u>*Gail, my donor has graciously agreed to give her perspective:*</u>

"*I have always believed in organ donation with my first driver's license having the heart stamp implanted on it. With every renewal there was no doubt that I would continue to indicate this desire. Also, about ten years ago when I was donating blood I heard about the need for bone marrow donors and registered and have been on that list. I have never been called and it is my understanding that when I turned 61 last year I was removed from the list as is their protocol. I had never given much thought to donating an organ while I was alive, until Linda became very ill.*

I remember the call from my brother when Linda was in the hospital in Las Vegas and how upset and difficult it was for him. When I saw them a couple of months later at a nephews wedding, Tim and I went for a walk. I hoped this would give him the opportunity to confide in me and vent some of his emotions. You have to know our family, as this is not a comfortable action for any of my brothers. As we were walking, I told Tim, if Linda needed a kidney, I had two and she was welcome to one of them. That was three and a half years before the transplant took place.

I did not realize what challenges Linda would need to accomplish before receiving this gift. Over the years she made many life changes and continued to work towards being a kidney transplant candidate. We talked often and she kept me abreast of her progress. I reassured her that when she was ready there would be a kidney for her.

I believe in fate and life happens as it should with me making the best decisions I am capable of at any given time. I have been fortunate to enjoy extreme good health, part of that is my doing and part is just luck. At 61 I take no medications other than calcium and a yearly infusion for osteoporosis. My outlook on life is to do the best I can today and deal with tomorrow, tomorrow.

When Linda got the go-ahead to involve her donors, I told her I was taking it one step at a time. There were many tests; any one of them could eliminate me as a prospective donor. The procedure was that they would schedule a test and then wait for the results. If those results were ok, the next test would be scheduled. As I live in Indiana and Stanford is not just around the corner, I was allowed to do the majority of the testing right here in town and results were sent to Stanford. When they did the blood matching, my hospital did the blood draw and sent the blood to Stanford. This matching took months before they were satisfied and was ready for me to proceed with further testing. I finally completed all the tests that could be done locally and the remainders were to be completed at Stanford, which meant my going to California for about a week. At this point there seemed no rush from Stanford for this to happen and as it was coming up to six months since the first test my husband and I began making plans for the holidays and a cruise in January. Little did we know all that would change with one phone call!

Both Linda and I had different individual patient coordinators, so most of our information was shared between the two of us. When I would get scheduled for a test, I would call Linda and let her know and then let her know the results. She would keep me informed of her progress and anything that she heard. I shared with her that Stanford didn't seem in any hurry to schedule my final testing and about our plans to book a cruise in January. She made some inquiries and shortly after I was contacted by Stanford. This was the second week of November.

My coordinators and I were looking at available time for the remainder of the testing and it turned out to be the first week of December. As she started to explain the final tests which would be Monday, Tuesday and Wednesday, she said that if they were all ok, then surgery would be on that Friday. To say that I was surprised is a huge understatement. This changed everything for us, as I said before I was anticipating going to California for a week and then returning sometime later for the surgery. This also made it very real for me. This was the first time there had been any mention of possible timeframe for the surgery.

My husband, Dan, and I talked it over and after numerous calls with my coordinator about time frames and post-surgery expectations we decided that December 10th would be fine with us. I could not see asking Linda to wait until February and continue on dialysis until after we returned from our cruise. So we began to make plans to be in California for most of December. We were going to drive out there as we needed a vehicle and wanted to take our dog along.

The remaining tests went fine and on Thursday, December 9th we checked into the hospital. Throughout these final days of testing, each professional I met inquired as to my decision to donate my kidney. They wanted to ensure that I was making this decision of my own free will and no one had coerced me to do this... I had agreed to participate in a study for Stanford so most of the evening I was busy with that. I don't remember feeling nervous or afraid and slept well. The next morning they came and got me early to go to surgery, Dan and my daughter,

Gayleen, accompanied me. I remember going to the OR and moving onto the table then I woke up in my room. While I don't remember a lot of pain I was very nauseous and it took a while before that got under control. I stayed in the hospital until Monday and then we continued to stay close to Stanford in a hotel for the remainder of the week. I didn't have stiches but was "super glued" and finding a comfortable position to sleep was difficult. But the biggest issue for me was that I was unable to pick up my dog, Breezy. This would continue for two months post-surgery.

There was one more challenge for us; the doctors would not allow me to drive back to Indiana unless I was given a daily blood thinner injection. I did not want to give this to myself so my husband took on that task. The first one was a little nerve racking but after that they went fine. We arrived home January first, and as I only worked part-time, I was back at work Monday, January 3rd. I continued to heal and was thrilled when the band of lifting anything over 10 pounds ended. Breezy was excited as well.

Prior to the actual surgery, not many people outside my immediate family knew I was going to donate a kidney. This was done for two reasons; 1) what if one of the tests was not ok, 2) I didn't want people to think that I was doing anything special. I was just following my belief; that we should do what we can to make life better for those we care about. My family understood this and they were supportive of my decision.

I continue to live my life as before; physically I am no different than prior to surgery other than I only have one kidney and now I have a scar down the front of my belly. It thrills me to chat with Linda and see how well she is doing and how she continues to progress. Just recently one of my daughter's close friends was diagnosed with kidney problems and Gayleen told me she had offered a kidney if needed. Based on my experience and Linda's success, I applaud her decision and hope many more people consider joining the ranks of living kidney donors."

Gail Bridges-Rea

Remember there are over 500,000 dialysis patients in the United States

<u>You can make a difference in family member, a friend, or even a stranger's life.</u>

If you are interested in becoming a living donor, please contact Stanford's living donor coordinator at 650-736-0795 to get the process started.

There is also a need for people to direct their organs for transplantation upon their death. Many people have this notification on their driver's license. If you would wish to make this a directive, please contact your local Department of Motor Vehicles.

CHAPTER 22

There were two areas I knew that I wanted to explore after my kidney transplant; one was writing this book and the other was volunteering in some capacity with the Stanford's transplant program and increasing the awareness of the need for both living donors. I have let the kidney transplant team at Stanford know that I am available to assist them in any way that they need.

I had made several attempts at writing this book and was not sure in which direction I should go. I did not know where to begin, what areas I should cover or how far back I should go. I read articles online, I glanced through books at the book stores, and still I had no idea. Just about the time I decided to give up on the idea, I received a flyer in the mail regarding adult classes that were being offered through a local night school. I read through to see what class I might want to take and saw that there was a class called, *"Writing Your Memoirs"*. I never thought of this as my "memoirs"; I thought only famous people wrote their memoirs. But I decided I would give the class a try, so I sent in my registration. The class was to begin in three weeks and last for five.

The first night of the class, I was surprised to see only three other students. What an interesting group -- Sophie, a young lady from Germany who was going to be in the US for one year, Edie, a retired professor from San Francisco State University and Bilge, a lady who moved to the US from Turkey. Each of us had a different story we wanted to tell.

The first thing the teacher said after he introduced himself was, *"I am not going to teach you anything in this class."* He went on to say that we were going to learn was from each other. I thought to myself, then why are we paying you – you should be paying us to be here. And to top it off, we had to pay an additional $25 to purchase his book from which he wasn't going to teach us. This book only proved to be <u>his</u> memoirs and was in no way a textbook.

He went around the room and asked each of us what specific area we wanted to write about. I told him I wanted to talk about the seven months prior to my being diagnosed with End Stage Renal Disease (ESRD) and the time that followed. He said then that is where I should start.

I learned all I needed to know in the first 15 minutes of the class, where to begin this book. I do give him credit for that because at least then I knew where to start. However, I had no idea where to go from there. So I sat down and started writing from my heart to see where that would take me.

I want people to realize that they needed to be their own advocate. That they can stand up for themselves. It is their right to question things when they do not understand and to demand answers until they did. It takes a lot of determination and courage for people to get where they want to go; and to not let anyone tell them their dreams and aspirations cannot be fulfilled.

Everyone has obstacles in their lives. It is how they choose to confront them that matters. Some people may choose to go around them, others may choose to ignore them and then there are those who choose to confront them head-on. There is no right or wrong answers when it comes to these obstacles. It is what a person chooses to get out of life.

My choices were my own decisions. After I was diagnosed with ESRD and was basically told I was going to die, I chose to "fight to live". My first step was to be positive. By making this choice I had to confront each obstacle I encountered. Sometimes I would overcome the obstacles on my own; sometimes I required assistance from others, however, it always started with me.

- When I was told by a UC Davis transplant surgeon that I would never be eligible for a transplant, I had to prove her wrong. It took over three years, and a lot of determination and help from others to overcome this obstacle.
- When I knew that I had to get stronger. I chose to learn how to swim.
- When I was unable to get the assistance I felt I needed from UCSF, I had to find an alternative. I called Stanford and with the help of Dr. Melcher I was able to obtain the tools I needed to make my dream of a kidney transplant a reality.
- When I was told after losing 190 pounds and was unable to lose the additional weight on my own, Dr. Melcher and Dr. Lau helped me find a way to by having the sleeve gastrectomy. That along with swimming nearly every day got me to the point of eligibility for my kidney transplant.

I have been asked if I was afraid of having the transplant surgery. Surprisingly enough, I was not. I had so much faith and confidence in Dr. Melcher and the staff at Stanford, I was never afraid. I realized how serious this operation was and I knew the risks. I also knew the benefits of having this surgery. With all of the extra skin I had from the weight that I lost, it increased the chances of infection. During the transplant surgery, Dr. Melcher removed five pounds of extra skin that was near the entry point where the kidney was going to be placed. This helped to lessen the risk of infection; however, the risks still remained. There was never a doubt in my mind that everything was going to turn out fine. This was my opportunity to have a chance at life without depending on dialysis.

So I did what the doctors told me to do. I continue to have my lab work done as scheduled, I keep all of my doctor's appointments, I take my medication as prescribed and I exercise regularly. When Dr. Kim advised me to take two showers a day to lessen the chance of infection, I took two showers a day. When I was told to have my bandage changed at least two times a day, Tim changed my bandages two times a day, sometimes three if it needed it. I followed whatever instructions I was given. My reward was I never developed any type of infections. I did whatever the doctors advised. Everyone's choice in life is their own. My hope for this book is to be able to help people realize their goals and dreams, whatever they may be.

If this book can help just one person then I have accomplished what I set out to do by writing this book.

Now it is time to begin a new ***Amazing Journey***.

GLOSSARY

CCU: Cardiac Care Unit

CKD: Chronic Kidney Disease

Desensitization:
Patients are said to be sensitization when they have developed organ rejection antibodies after transfusion, previous transplant or pregnancy. Prior to surgery, an intravenous immunoglobulin (IVIG) infusion can help highly sensitization patients accept a new kidney.

Dialysis:
A procedure used to filter off waste products from the blood and remove surplus fluid from the body in someone who has kidney failure.

End Stage Renal Disease (ESRD): Kidney failure, requiring dialysis.

Fellow: A medical doctor on a fellowship to specialize in a specific area.

Nephrologist: A doctor who specializes in kidney disease.

PCP: Primary Care Physician

In the Beginning of the journey – July 2007

and now November 2011

www.ingramcontent.com/pod-product-compliance
Lightning Source LLC
LaVergne TN
LVHW041616070526
838199LV00052B/3172